NATIVE NORTH AMERICA

LIVING WISDOM

NATIVE NORTH AMERICA

LARRY J. ZIMMERMAN
ASSOCIATE AUTHOR: BRIAN LEIGH MOLYNEAUX

SERIES CONSULTANT: **PIERS VITEBSKY**

DBP
• • •

DUNCAN BAIRD PUBLISHERS

LONDON

Native North America

First published in Great Britain in 1996 by Macmillan Reference Books.

Conceived, created and designed by Duncan Baird Publishers. This edition published by Duncan Baird Publishers Sixth Floor Castle House 75–76 Wells Street London W1P 3RE

10 9 8 7 6 5 4 3 2 1

Editor: Peter Bently
Editorial coordinators: Daphne Bien Tebbe, Kirsty Seymour-Ure
Designer: Steve Painter
Design assistant: Richard Horsford
Picture research: Jan Croot and Photosearch Inc., New York

Typeset in Times NR MT.
Colour reproduction by Colourscan, Singapore.
Printed in Singapore by Imago Publishing Limited.

Contents

Introduction

Native North Americans are among the most culturally diverse populations on earth, yet also among the most stereotyped by outsiders. Thus, in the 18th century, Native people were characterized as "noble savages", while today's environmentalists call them "the first ecologists". In old Hollywood Westerns, Indians are often portrayed as bloodthirsty savages. More recently, the film *Dances With Wolves* presents Indians as peace-loving victims of "progress".

Contradictory representations such as these expose the ambivalence inherent in white attitudes toward Indians. On the one hand, whites see themselves as greatly more advanced: white society is sophisticated, civilized and modern; Indian society is primitive and traditional. Yet whites also see Indians as naturally wise and close to the earth, possessing a way of life that respects the planet.

Native peoples have different reactions to different white perceptions. Most understandably reject images that emphasize savagery. They are also suspicious of those who, as they see it, take Indian beliefs out of context and incorporate them in "New Age" belief systems. On the other hand, it is unlikely that many Indians resent their cultures being seen by some outsiders as models for environmental salvation.

Indians lay great emphasis on respect. To be respectful, non-Indians should not pry too deeply into what Indians hold sacred, or exploit Indian beliefs in their own quests for spiritual redemption. Non-Indians should be wary of assuming that they know what Indians think. For example, liberal whites may scrupulously avoid the word "Indian", but it is

perfectly satisfactory to many Native people. The Native activist Russell Means (see p.33) argues that "Indian" is acceptable because, he claims, Columbus described aboriginal Americans not as *Indios* ("people of India") but as people *In Dios* ("in God").

To show respect, non-Indians must also accept that Indians have valid ways of knowing the world that are different from those proposed by Western science and history. Indians are entitled to ignore archaeological theories about their origins that deny oral traditions possibly millennia old. Westerners take the voice of science for granted, but Indians who reject their own version of who they are and where they came from take a step toward cultural extinction.

Indians, like any group or culture, do not possess a monopoly of truth about

themselves. However, non-Indians must understand that their own knowledge of Indians has limits: they can know *about* Indians but can never assume that they know what it means to *be* Indian. Non-Indians are often unaware that Indians still exist at all. Native peoples are not mere artefacts of the past: they are very much present in the modern world. Native cultures possess a richness, flexibility and adaptability that can never be conveyed by crude stereotyping. It is precisely these qualities that have enabled Indians to survive the traumatic five centuries since whites first set foot on North American soil.

A view of Valley of Fire, Nevada, now a State Park but formerly part of the territory of the Southern Paiutes before they were dispossessed by whites in the 19th century (see pp.50–51).

The First American Peoples

According to the holy people, North America was never an empty land. It came into being when the first humans scrambled up to the surface from other worlds within the womb of the earth, or descended from parallel worlds that existed above the sky. Whether they lived on the rocky coasts or on the vast, endless plain, in the forests of the Northeast or the deserts of the Southwest, each group recognized its own spiritual homeland, a place where the people could see the evidence of their beginnings.

Archaeologists searching for the origins of the earliest North American cultures have found the remains of hearths, animal bones and distinctive, finely-flaked stone tools more than 10,000 years old. They were left by hunters whose forebears had followed mammoths and other large animals of the last Ice Age from Asia into the Americas. During the great freeze, sea levels sank so low that what are now Siberia and Alaska were linked by a stretch of land that scientists call Beringia. Hunting bands probably ranged freely back and forth across Beringia before it was claimed once more by the sea. Only very gradually did the hunters penetrate deeper into the Americas. However, by *c.*8000BC, human beings had established themselves in almost every part of the continent.

Evidence of the presence of early North Americans is widespread in prehistoric petroglyphs throughout the continent. These handprint designs are on a rock at Galisteo Basin, New Mexico. Possibly up to 2,000 years old, their purpose remains a mystery.

Identity

Native North America has a confusion of names and identities, reflecting the tumultuous events of the last 500 years of aboriginal history. The people referred to as Ojibway, Ojibwa or Chippewa, for example, call themselves Anishinabe, and Arctic hunters known around the world as Eskimos might speak of themselves as Inuit or Aleut.

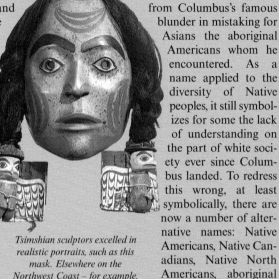

Tsimshian sculptors excelled in realistic portraits, such as this mask. Elsewhere on the Northwest Coast – for example, among the Haida – there was less emphasis on individual identity.

The names by which Native groups refer to themselves recall a time when the land was a mosaic of societies that had developed over thousands of years. Identity was strong and exclusive, because each group lived in its own world, with a distinct territory and language or dialect, and unique traditions. Many names of tribes and nations, such as Anishinabe and Inuit, can roughly be translated as, simply, "the people".

Many groups acquired their tribal names only recently from white missionaries, explorers and traders, who were struck by distinct characteristics of people such as the Nez Perce (French: "Pierced Nose"). Europeans sometimes adopted names used by other groups. "Sioux", from the Ojibway for "snake", means "enemies". Modern Inuit dislike "Eskimo", an Algonquian word meaning "eaters of raw meat", not because it is incorrect, but rather because it was conferred by a traditional enemy.

The term "Indian" derives from Columbus's famous blunder in mistaking for Asians the aboriginal Americans whom he encountered. As a name applied to the diversity of Native peoples, it still symbolizes for some the lack of understanding on the part of white society ever since Columbus landed. To redress this wrong, at least symbolically, there are now a number of alternative names: Native Americans, Native Canadians, Native North Americans, aboriginal people, Native people and First Nations people. However, these names are largely used by governments and the liberal white middle class. Most Native people, sensitive to their own specific identities, prefer to use tribal names, and many also freely call themselves Indians. The experience of Tom Hudson (Black Wolf's Shadow), an Ojibway Vietnam veteran, is not untypical: "When I was a kid, I was called a Half Breed ... around the age of 15, I was just called Breed. When I got out of the Army, I was called a Native American. When I was in my 30s, I was called a Native North American. When I was over 35, I was called a Native North American with aboriginal rights. Now that I am over 40, I think it would be nice if people would just call me Tom!" The point is that what to call Indians is a decision for Indians themselves.

The question of Native identity is now an important social issue involving a complex interweaving of ancestry, politics, economics and spirituality. It is complicated today by the intermixing of tribal groups and the injection through intermarriage of European, African and Asian blood. One group, the Métis, a people with an identifiable history and material culture in Canada, was produced by the union of French fur traders with Native women. The Métis are still fighting for status as an aboriginal people. Native identity may also be subject to legal tests. The US government has introduced a controversial law allowing only Native Americans to produce Native American crafts. This law's definition of Native American depends not on ethnic ancestry, but on acceptance as an Indian by a legally-constituted tribe or nation.

Being a Native North American is therefore a question of social identification and sympathy, involving participation in a certain kind of life and a particular view of the past and future. It lies more in a personal commitment to an identity extending back thousands of years, than in the superficial trappings of "Indianness", such as its popularized rituals, religions and modes of dress.

Many white educators in North America aimed to eradicate Indian identity altogether and to accomplish the complete assimilation of Native peoples into the dominant European society. The Carlisle Indian Industrial School, founded by Richard H. Pratt in 1879 at Carlisle, Pennsylvania, was one of the leading institutions for "civilizing" Indians. These photographs show Tom Torlino, a Navajo, before and after his admission to the school (see also p.25).

Concepts of time

A European conceives of the past as a long straight road leading backward from the here and now to a distant invisible point on the horizon. This outlook makes the past a remote and foreign place, distancing people from the ancients, including their own ancestors. However, many Indian groups conceive of the passage of time not as linear but as circular, marked by the birth, growth, maturity, death and regeneration of all things that share the earth – plants, animals, people. This pattern is echoed in the rising and setting of the sun and the lunar and solar cycles. The past is a place where all things reside that have completed the cycle. All things are "out there" now, not distant but immanent.

For Native North Americans, irrespective of cultural tradition, the rising and setting of the sun form the basic rhythm of daily life, just as it does for most peoples. Indians chart the passage of longer periods in a diversity of ways, often observing a natural calendar whose markers are the changes in the world around them. For example, the spawning of the salmon is a key seasonal marker for peoples of the Northwest Coast, while desert dwellers note the ripening of the fruit of the saguaro cactus (see p.112). In many cultures, communal life follows the rhythms of nature. For example, the Iroquois peoples traditionally celebrate the coming of spring, summer and autumn, respectively, on the occasions of the flowing of the maple sap (February to March), the first strawberries (June) and the maturing of the corn (maize) crop (October).

It is probable also that some peoples measured time by observing the positions of heavenly bodies. For example, the enigmatic "medicine wheels" of the northern Plains may have been used to chart astronomical events (see p.77).

Battles between Indians and US troops, depicted on the tipi of a 19th-century Kiowa chief. The Indian artist felt no need to represent events in linear, chronological sequence.

A shaft of sunlight falls onto a spiral and cross etched on a rock by prehistoric Anasazi peoples near present-day Tuba City, Arizona. Such "sundials" may have helped to determine the time for planting and other agricultural events. Among the Hopi, a "sun watcher" observes the rising sun every day to establish when the solstices occur. The time of the last frosts is calculated from the winter solstice.

THE LIVING PAST

Many Indians believe that the ancestors and other ancient beings are never far from the living or from each other. When a person dies, he or she joins the ancestors in another state of being within the present. Where a European might say "My grandfather lived in the 20th century and Sitting Bull in the 19th century", an Indian would say "Grandfather and Sitting Bull are here now".

Many Native groups are reminded of the living presence of the ancients in stories and works of art. For example, the peoples of the Northwest Coast lived in a world that was saturated with visual representations of Raven (see p.123), Killer Whale and other sacred ancestral beings, many of whom were responsible for the great events that formed the world and the people. They were constantly present in images carved on totem poles, houses, canoes, fine clothing, dance costumes, masks, ceremonial dishes and everyday housewares.

Totem poles at the Tsimshian village of Kitwancool in British Columbia displayed images of ancestral clan culture heroes.

The peopling of North America

Traces of the lives of the earliest inhabitants of North America are often buried beneath layers of soil accumulated over thousands of years. Signs of an early human presence – chipped stone tools, animal bones, firepits and other remains – are rarely discovered: they might be unearthed as a result of the erosion of the sides of a valley, or found by chance under debris in rock shelters and caves. Nevertheless, every discovery helps archaeologists to create a picture of human life on the continent at the time of the last Ice Age.

The current physical evidence indicates that more than 10,000 years ago, hunting peoples were living in several widely separated regions: the Northeast, the western Plains and Southwest, and northern Alaska. This ancient world was sparsely populated by small groups who hunted mammoth, mastodon, giant bison and many medium-sized and smaller animals, such as deer and rabbits. The hunters lived in temporary dwellings and moved according to the availability of game. They pursued a way of life that was to be found

This map shows the extent of the ice caps during the "Wisconsin" period, the final great glacial advance of the last Ice Age. So much water was locked up in the ice caps that the sea level fell to expose a strip of land linking Siberia to Alaska across the Bering Straits. It was across this strip – known as Beringia – that people are thought to have wandered from northeast Asia into North America and gradually spread out over the continent. The migration routes, which are highly speculative, show how people might have moved into the interior of the continent along ice-free corridors during brief periods of thaw.

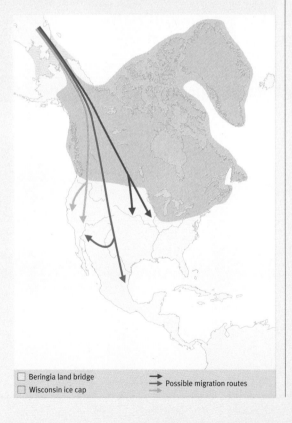

☐ Beringia land bridge
☐ Wisconsin ice cap

➡ Possible migration routes

WEAPONS FOR BIG GAME HUNTERS

The North American hunters of the so-called Palaeo-Indian era – the period immediately following the last Ice Age – developed effective weapons to hunt the mammoth, giant bison and other large, thick-skinned animals that provided them with food and, presumably, other resources such as hides. The hunters developed two main types of stone point, known as Clovis and Folsom after two sites in New Mexico. The stone was finely chipped from the centre toward the edges on both sides in order to form a slender and very sharp arrow or spearhead. The base of the point was finely fluted so that it could be firmly attached to a shaft.

A stone spearhead lies between the ribs of a giant bison killed 10,000 years ago. The spearhead was discovered near Folsom, New Mexico.

until recent times deep in the subarctic forests of northern Canada.

The oldest human remains found in the Americas belong to a much later period than the oldest remains found in Asia. During the last Ice Age, the Beringia land bridge effectively made North America and Asia a single continent. These facts, coupled with the general physical similarity of Native North American and northern Asian peoples, suggest that the mammoth-hunters may have moved into the Americas from the west. Although the great ice caps covered most of the north during the last Ice Age, periods of slightly warmer weather at various times in the past 40,000 years opened up ice-free corridors into the interior of the continent, one probably along the coast and one or more running parallel with the eastern edge of the Rocky Mountains. The possibility of migration across Beringia came to an end as the climate warmed, the ice retreated for the last time and the land bridge was submerged by the rising sea.

The theory that the human occupa-tion of the continent was relatively recent is based on the absence of sites in North America that can be securely dated from before 15,000BC. However, evidence from South America suggests that the pattern of human occupation of the Americas may have been much more complex. In the far south, in Patagonia, there are sites that were occupied as early as any in North America: humans must therefore have migrated into North America consider-ably earlier than this. Recent excava-tions in Brazil are even more surprising: they have yielded artefacts which, archaeologists there suggest, may be more than 30,000 years old. This implies that humans may have first moved into North America at a time when there was no land bridge. Cer-tainly, the absence of a land bridge did not prevent seafaring Asian Arctic peo-ples – ancestors of the Inuit – from set-tling the northern coasts of Alaska and Canada several thousand years later. However, there is no absolutely firm evi-dence of a human presence in North

America before *c*.15,000BC.

The presence or absence of datable evidence is not the only issue at stake when discussing the peopling of North America. Europeans, who are accustomed to scientific solutions, tend to favour the migration theories derived from the systematic analysis of sites, artefacts, chronological tables and maps. In accepting the scientific view, it is tempting to overlook the undoubted fact that the first North Americans never thought of themselves as migrants who left one continent for a new life in another. They simply lived as they had always done, moving from place to place in pursuit of game.

There is another explanation of the human presence in America: that people have occupied the land since the beginning of time. This idea occurs in many Native traditions and remains a religious and political issue to this day. The mythologies of many present-day Indian peoples, such as the Ojibway and Hopi (see box below), recount how the first people wandered from a place of origin to their eventual homeland. Origin stories (see pp.116–19) may also reflect a people's way of life. For example, the creation stories of settled farming peoples, such as the Pueblo Indians,

Native hunting methods were perfected over thousands of years of adaptation to the American environment. In this watercolour of 1585 by the English artist-explorer John White, North Carolina Indians are shown using traditional fishing equipment, including spears, nets and fish traps, to exploit the abundant natural resources of the coastal waters.

THE HOPI MIGRATION STORY

According to the Hopi, the first people migrated upward through three worlds, eventually emerging in this, the Fourth World.

Másaw, their guardian spirit, told them to migrate north, south, east and west until they reached the sea, and then to retrace their steps to find their common homeland. Not all clans completed the journey. Some stayed in the

THIS PAGE AND OPPOSITE Migration spirals depicted in Hopi rock art.

tell of emergence from the earth at precise places in the landscape. The creation stories of many traditional hunting and gathering peoples reflect their traditional questing lives, searching for game or seeking visions. These stories often recount how a number of beings dived to the bottom of a great sea in quest of soil from which to form the first land (see p.117).

As the climate warmed and became drier, the glaciers and tundra retreated to the north, to be replaced by grasslands and forests. The giant Ice Age animals disappeared – some scientists think that they were hunted to extinction. People adopted a more generalized hunting and gathering lifestyle. Inventions such as the bow and arrow and pottery appeared several thousand years later and, in places where the climate was suitable and the soil fertile, people were able to produce corn (maize), beans and other crops. With the introduction of agriculture, fertile valleys, such as those of the Mississippi and Ohio rivers, furnished the successive Adena, Hopewell and Mississippian cultures with the resources and energy to build large towns, raise great earth monuments, create spectacular art and develop elaborate religious beliefs.

In other places, humans hunted, fished and gathered as they had always done.

The peoples of North America were by no means static and isolated in the thousands of years before the arrival of Europeans. They traded materials such as stone (for tools) and shells (for ornamentation) over great distances. As groups moved from place to place, languages multiplied and spread. The scale of activity in these times is seen in the way that speakers of related languages are now separated by huge distances. For example, the Navajo and Apache languages of the Southwest are related to the languages of hunters in Alaska and the Yukon (see pp.164–5).

On the eve of the European invasion, therefore, North America was a place where humans had thrived for at least 15,000 years and perhaps much longer. The changes that followed, which were to have such a devastating impact on Native peoples, were due in part to the vast differences in perception that still divide aboriginal cultures from Europeans. As far as Native North Americans were concerned, the land was occupied, managed and familiar. But the white explorers and settlers saw nothing but empty wilderness, waiting to be conquered.

tropics and others lost their way. Those who returned symbolized their migrations by two types of spiral: square, representing their turning back at the seas, and round, showing how they wandered ever closer to their home.

The whole pattern traced by the people's journeys forms a great cross, *Túwanasavi* (Centre of the Universe), whose centre is in the present-day Hopi homeland.

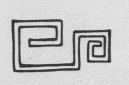

Cahokia

The largest settlement in North America before the beginning of the 19th century was a complex of mounds, plazas, palisades and residential areas near the Mississippi River, seven miles (11.2km) from present-day St Louis, Missouri. This urban area, now called Cahokia, covered over five square miles (13km^2), and developed from a small farming village established sometime between AD600 and AD800. The people planted corn (maize) in the fertile soil of the floodplain, just as the Hopewell inhabitants of the region (see pp.39–40) had done before them. But the Cahokians had hybrid varieties of corn, similar to those grown in Mexico, that were hardier and produced larger crops. With this wealth in corn, Cahokia, along with other villages on the Mississippi and its tributaries, thrived and expanded.

Each of these Mississippian settlements was organized around large earth mounds and plazas, features strikingly similar to the temple and plaza complexes of Mesoamerica. One settlement, at Moundville, Alabama, had 20 mounds arranged in a circle. Some were for burials, others were temples and élite residences. In Wisconsin, a 20-acre (8-ha) fortified town, Aztalan, stood beside a series of massive animal and bird effigy mounds built along the river by an earlier culture. But Cahokia was the most sophisticated urban centre north of Mexico.

When the Spanish travelled up the Mississippi in the 16th century, Cahokia had long been abandoned. A possible cause of Cahokia's decline, and of the decline of the Mississippian towns as a whole, was overpopulation leading to epidemics, social strife and drought.

Cahokia Creek

North Plaza

Merrel Plaza

Woodhenge

Monks Mound

Central Plaza

Twin Mounds

Monumental mounds   Populated area

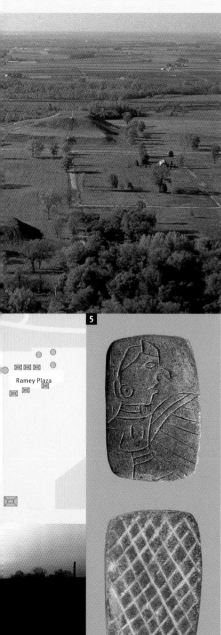

Pacific Ocean

Colorado River

Mississippi

Rio Grande

● CAHOKIA MOUNDS

North Atlantic Ocean

1 *A modern view of Cahokia. At its peak, between AD850 and 1150, the city had over 100 flat-topped pyramids and earthen mounds, of which about 20 are still visible. Large wooden structures – probably high-status residences – once stood on the mounds, but most citizens lived in smaller wooden buildings around the mounds and plazas. The population may have been over 10,000, and as many as 40,000 people may have lived in outlying villages.*

2 *A plan of the city, showing the extent of the urban area and the principal plazas, mounds and dwellings. The largest mound, the so-called Monks Mound, rose 100 feet (30m) above the central plaza and supported a wattle-and-daub building with a thatched roof – either a temple or the home of a ruler or religious leader.*

3 *The ring of stakes, or woodhenge (see plan; this is a modern reconstruction* in situ*), was probably a solar calendar, used to determine the dates of important festivals and religious ceremonies. The henge consisted of a central pole and an outer ring, including the so-called "solstice pole", immediately behind and to its left in the photo (marked with a white band).*

4 *At dawn on the summer solstice, the "solstice pole" and the central pole of the woodhenge are in exact alignment with the sun as it appears above the Monks Mound. The main mounds of the site stand along the same alignment.*

5 *The two sides of a clay tablet, one of thousands of artefacts found at Cahokia. It is known as the "Birdman Tablet" from the figure depicted on one side, who may be a deity or a priest. Similar figures have been discovered on objects found at other Mississippian sites.*

Ramey Plaza

5

Dispossession

The first European incursions into North America were belittled by the sheer size of the continent. Small groups of Vikings and Basque fishermen on the northeast coast, and the first Spanish, French and English explorers, did little to disturb thousands of years of culture. When the first small European trading posts, missions and settlements appeared, they were like tiny islands in a great sea of wilderness.

But when Europeans planted flags they laid claim to the land itself, and within 400 years they had completely dispossessed the aboriginal people. Although some Native groups controlled hunting or gathering grounds, and all respected the boundaries of sacred places, none had any concept of territory as lines on a map – divided, bought and sold. The settlers, however, imposed this alien concept with ruthless vigour.

There were three types of European invasion: physical (the occupation of territory by immigrants), spiritual (the imposition of Christianity) and material (the introduction of goods such as guns and alcohol). Native people were driven out, swindled by unobserved treaties, subjugated, shattered, plied with alcohol and confined to reservations. But their culture was not destroyed. Under the influence of inspired leaders, traditional Native cultures have survived into the modern world.

This Portuguese map of 1546 shows the St Lawrence River ("Rio do Canada") and Jacques Cartier (in black and red), who explored the region 1534–42 and claimed it for France. South is at top.

Forced movements

The displacement of Native North Americans from their homelands was subtle at first. Missions and trading posts from New France (northeast Canada) to Florida distracted Indian people from the encroachments of the settlers with the lure of ready-made cloth, kettles, guns, knives and other useful goods. The first settlers were attracted to fertile, well-watered land close to navigable waterways, and it was not long before the coastal areas and river valleys quickly became out of bounds to the Indians.

The demand for Indian slaves in the English colonies of America and on sugar plantations in the West Indies forced many small southern coastal tribes to flee inland. Compelled to compete for diminishing land and resources, Indian groups preyed on one another. Enticed by pay-offs in trade goods, they often joined forces with the settlers. In 1704, James Moore, the British governor of Carolina, marched into Spanish-held Florida with a band of colonists and a thousand Creek, Apalachicola and Yuchi Indians. They almost wiped out the Apalachee, Timucua and Calusa people – who had already suffered under the brutal Spanish occupation – and returned home with more than 6,000 captives for the slave market.

Further north, the pressure of European settlement and competition in the lucrative fur trade also caused conflict among the Indian tribes. Armed by the

Dutch and English, the Iroquois League (see p.41) dispersed the Huron and pushed the Ojibway into Sioux territory in the western Great Lakes; the Ojibway in turn pushed the Sioux into the Plains. The Iroquois lost their homeland after the American War of Independence (1775–83), fleeing to British Canada as the victorious United States consolidated its hold on the territory. But in Canada, too, Indian land effectively ceased to exist as the Crown assumed ownership of all land, regardless of the rights of the aboriginal inhabitants.

In 1787, the US Congress passed the Northwest Ordinance, which declared that "[the Indians'] lands and property shall never be taken from them without

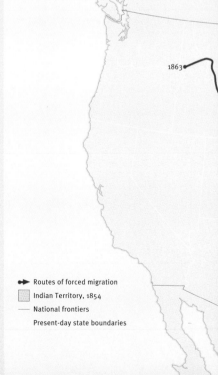

This map shows some of the most notable – or notorious – forced relocations of Native American peoples, with the dates of their first removal from their homelands and of their final resettlement in the Indian Territory.

➡ Routes of forced migration

▢ Indian Territory, 1854

— National frontiers

Present-day state boundaries

1863

their consent". The continuing presence of Indians, however, was felt to be a hindrance to white settlement, and these fine words soon rang hollow. From the Carolinas to California, small Native groups were sometimes exterminated by gangs or driven away. The official solution, initially, was to remove them from areas earmarked for white settlers to small plots of marginal land. In 1830, President Andrew Jackson went further with the Indian Removal Act, which compelled all Native people to move west of the Mississippi, leaving the east to the whites. In theory, the Indians were to live freely in their own "Indian Territory", but in practice, westward white expansion forged ahead unabated.

As soon as their lands were required by settlers, Indians were generally forced onto reservations (see pp.24–5).

Resistance to the trauma of dislocation was met with harsh military action. For example, when the Navajo fought back in the 1850s, the New Mexico Volunteers, led by Colonel Kit Carson, ravaged their country. In 1864, the Navajo surrendered after a last stand at their sacred site of Canyon de Chelly. More than 8,000 people – most on foot – were forced to cross 300 miles (480km) of mountain and desert to Fort Sumner, New Mexico. Many died en route. After several years of intense suffering, the survivors were allowed to return to a reservation within their original lands.

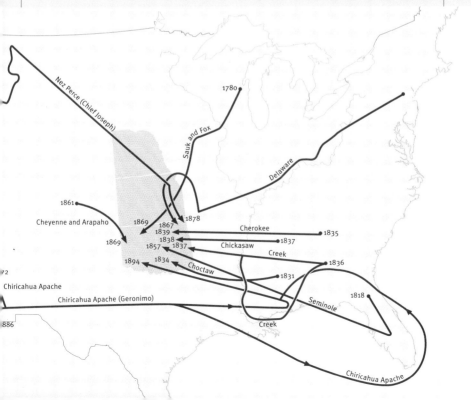

Reservations

The establishment of reservations during the period of white expansion aimed at first to keep Indians entirely apart from white society. Later, it was hoped that the marginalization of Native culture would hasten the assimilation of the Indians into the dominant society.

The concept of reserved areas for Indians originated in the "praying towns" of the 17th century (see p.27). The first reservations in the more modern sense were created in the Northeast in the first decades after US independence. They tended to be portions of a group's homeland, but as the white demand for land increased, the authorities abandoned all pretence of retaining tribal integrity. Thousands of years of

cultural adaptation to particular environments were nullified in just a few decades as Native farmers and forest peoples were resettled in unfamiliar terrain, usually on marginal land.

In 1825, the US government envisaged a permanent solution to the "Indian question" in the form of a vast Indian Country west of the Mississippi. Officially known as Indian Territory from 1834, the proposed territory covered present-day Kansas, Oklahoma and parts of Nebraska, Colorado and Wyoming. The first reservations there were for the five displaced peoples of the Southeast (see p.45). For a time they thrived, achieving a level of economic prosperity and literacy greater than that

Members of the Rosebud Sioux tribe wait for the federal government's issue of beef on the Rosebud Reservation in the southern part of Dakota Territory (present-day South Dakota) in the early 1890s. The Sioux were among the last peoples to put up armed resistance to their removal to reservations.

SCHOOLS FOR INDIANS

Western-style schools were established on most Indian reservations, but in order to speed up assimilation Indian boarding schools were also set up across the US and Canada. Children were taken from their homes and kept at these schools for most of the year, often until adulthood. The goal, as the founder of the Carlisle Indian School in Pennsylvania put it, was to "kill the Indian ... and save the man". Pupils had to learn English, adopt Christianity, study Western subjects and reject their native dress, language and religion. A few successfully absorbed white culture, but most left with little more than a profoundly confused cultural identity.

The mission school on the Seneca Reservation near Niagara Falls, 1821. At this time, reservation school pupils still wore traditional dress.

of some neighbouring states. But the disruption of the US Civil War in the 1860s brought economic ruin. By the end of the war, tribes were forced to agree to new treaties and to give up land to Comanche, Kiowa and Cheyenne groups, and to peoples removed from the north. The future Oklahoma became a dumping ground for more than 65 disparate tribes and bands – farmers, hunters, friends, enemies and strangers alike (see map, pp.22–3).

White settlement encroached on the Indian Territory even before the Civil War. The "inviolable" Indian lands were gradually organized as states, and when Oklahoma achieved statehood in 1907 the Indian Territory ceased to exist. By 1975 Oklahoma's 29 tribes controlled only 65,000 acres (26,000ha).

The loss of territory was hastened by the allotment of tribal lands to individual owners, a measure that aimed to speed up Indian assimilation. The Dawes General Allotment Act of 1887 sought to break up tribal lands into small plots of at most 160 acres (64ha), a policy alien to Indian traditions of communality. The result was the loss of 95 million acres (38 million ha) of reservation. A final attempt to dismantle reservations came in 1953, when Congress resolved to buy back reservation lands. Before this policy fell out of favour, 19 tribes lost more than 2.5 million acres (1 million ha) of land.

The trend has been reversed in recent decades with the settlement of some land claims. There have been notable settlements in Canada, which historically had followed, although less harshly than in the US, a similar process of confining Indians to reserves. Under an agreement finalized in the early 1990s, the Northwest Territories are to be divided between Indians (the Dene and Métis) in the west and the Inuit in the east. (See also map, pp.170–71.)

The impact of Christianity

The Huron were suspicious of the French Jesuits – strange, black-robed, celibate men bearing gifts and the promise of eternal life. The Jesuits lived in Huron villages and learned the Huron language, but they did not want to live Huron lives. They rejected Indian spirituality and urged people to accept the teachings of an alien religion.

Although the Christian God was a great spirit, and so compatible with the beliefs of some Indians, the sacred figures of the Christian story lived in a land that was unimaginable and distant, rather than in territory that the tribe knew and could enter. Christian teachings centred on a book that the Indians could not read, and were expressed in alien imagery, symbolism and music.

Nevertheless, the missionaries won converts. For many, Christianity was a matter of economic opportunism. The Huron found that adopting the trappings of French culture won them greater access to the fur trade. The prospect of an alliance with the French prompted Membertou, a Micmac chief, to be baptized together with several members of his family by the French missionary Recollets in 1610 at Port Royal in present-day Nova Scotia.

Those who offered Christianity as a solution to the sufferings of Native peoples were the very settlers who had caused those sufferings in the first place. For the Timucua of Florida, conversion represented one means of easing the depredations of their vindictive Spanish overlords. Similarly, the Mohawk of the Northeast requested missionaries after the French destroyed their villages in a punitive raid in 1666.

Converts were required to reject traditional forms of belief and ritual – the essence of their culture and identity. The Puritan settlers of New England used force to ensure compliance. The Wampanoag, largely reduced to servitude by 1662, were prosecuted for hunting and fishing on the Sabbath, using Indian medicines and marrying outside the Christian church. In Plymouth, Massachusetts, Indians faced the death sentence for denying Christianity. William Duncan, a 19th-century Anglican lay minister, encouraged the Tsimshian of the Northwest Coast to destroy much of their heritage of masks, costumes and other religious regalia. Such actions were typical. In the United States, the Bureau of Indian Affairs issued a Code of Religious Offences in 1883 which banned, among other rituals, the Sun Dance (see p.112) as well as Native medical practices. At around the same time,

The Spanish church at Picuris in New Mexico was founded in 1621. Pueblo "converts" often practised traditional religion in secret.

the Canadian government banned the potlatch (see p.62).

Roman Catholicism proved to be a particularly strong force, because many of its features had familiar resonances for the converts: the cult of the Virgin recalled their own reverence for Mother Earth, the saints were not unlike Indian sacred beings, and dramatic ceremonialism was a feature of both Catholicism and many Indian cultures.

While Christianity took hold among some Native groups, for many peoples it failed to supplant traditional spirituality. For example, it said little about respect for the natural world, which was a central feature of many Native American traditions. Brought from a foreign land by people whose influence was not generally perceived as benign, Christianity remained essentially a foreign doctrine for most Indians.

PRAYING TOWNS

The task of converting Indians was often difficult, because outside the missions Native life continued unchanged. For conversion to be effective, converts had to be isolated from their traditional culture. In 1650 the English Puritan missionary John Eliot took this idea to its extreme. In keeping with the ideals of his own community, a religious colony, he established a "Red Puritan" settlement for his converts at Natick, south of Boston. Converts built the town in an English style, complete with a public meeting house and a footbridge over the local river. The townspeople replaced their hereditary leadership with elected representatives in the English manner, and outlawed such Native practices as polygamy, seasonal migration and shamanic curing.

The idea spread quickly along the coast and 20 more such "praying towns" sprang up. However, they lasted only until the devastating war between the Puritans and an alliance of Wampanoags and Narragansetts in 1675.

A Presbyterian missionary, Kate McBeth, with four Nez Perce converts at a mission in Idaho around the turn of the 20th century. As well as receiving religious instruction, Indians who attended McBeth's mission school were taught how to conduct themselves in polite white society.

Two faces of history

When Indian guides led the first European adventurers into the continent, they travelled up rivers and lakes in the same vessels, ate the same food and suffered equally the rigours of the environment. As fellow humans, they had identical physical needs, but their perceptions of the world about them were utterly different. A huge chasm separated their cultural outlooks.

Native people were no doubt amazed at their first sight of Europeans. An old Micmac tale of the coming of the white man recounts that the first European ships to appear on the horizon were thought to be floating islands with a few bare trees; some people even thought that they could make out bears climbing in the branches. The first European traders would have thrilled the natives with familiar objects in wonderful new materials: knives not of stone but of sharp steel; cooking vessels of copper that did not break in the fire; and beads of glass in endless vibrant colours. Guns were clearly magical. The swiftly-fired bow and silent arrow were better suited to the tactics of stealth and surprise favoured by Indian warriors than the loud, heavy, cumbersome muzzle-loading firearms brought by the first whites. But a bow was effective only at close range, while a gun could magically kill an enemy or an animal from afar in the blinking of an eye.

The driving force behind the great European voyages of discovery was rarely a curiosity to explore new lands and cultures. Far from it: the adventurers were motivated principally by the prospect of extending Europe's markets and resources. When Spanish, French, English and Russian explorers, traders and settlers encountered North America's native inhabitants, there was no question of reaching an accommodation with them. They came with the eyes of conquerors, who saw not a rich diversity of cultures but people who seemed to live rudimentary lives in poverty. They also saw an opportunity to exploit the land and its abundant resources.

The perception of Native people as economically deprived – when they had

The presence of Europeans in the Southwest was recorded, probably in the 16th century, by the Indian artist who produced these petroglyphs in the Canyon de Chelly, Arizona. The strange new beasts – horses – probably inspired the artist as much as their white riders, a Spanish friar and his companions.

THE IRON HORSE

European Americans saw the railway as a great advance in civilization. As so often, however, what the white man hailed as progress proved to be yet another nail in the coffin of the traditional Native way of life. Although many Indian tribes resisted the coming of the "iron horse" to their lands, by 1891 there were four railways spanning the US and one, the Canadian Pacific, across Canada. For Plains Indians who depended on bison meat, hide, bone and sinew for their livelihood, the impact was devastating, because buffalo hunting from the trains became a favourite travellers' sport. Between 1869, when

the Union and Central Pacific railroads linked up, and 1890, railborne hunters reduced the bison population from six million to barely a thousand.

A bison shoot from a train; an engraving of 1882. Railborne bison hunts became especially popular after the market for hides boomed in the 1870s.

---

lived successfully for countless generations in their homelands – was influenced by the notion that European material civilization represented the pinnacle of worldly achievement. Other peoples lagged behind, perhaps because they lived outside the sanction of God or because they belonged to a lower order of beings. This view seems to have underlain the attitude of Spaniard and English Puritan alike toward aboriginal North Americans well into the 18th century. Europeans were not impressed with how the natural world seemed to be an integral part of the culture and spirituality of the Indians.

An Iroquois comb carved by a Cayuga artist in the late 17th century. It depicts Europeans – perhaps French missionaries or traders associated with the establishment of the Sulpician and Jesuit missions in Cayuga territory in 1668.

Christian doctrine saw nature as a servant of humanity, to be controlled and conquered, not emulated or treated as an equal. In the mid-19th century, Charles Darwin's theory of evolution served to reinforce the European belief in the "baseness" of the Indians. They were judged to be either the degraded survivors of a once-great race, or a people whose evolution was less advanced than that of whites.

Therefore, at the core of relations between the aboriginal people and the whites, there was no common language or worldview and, little sense of common humanity, at least on the part of Europeans. As settlers flooded to their "New World" in increasing numbers, this lack of mutual understanding proved a tragedy for Native North Americans. Although there was some Native ownership of resource areas, the idea that land could be a personal possession was generally unintelligible. Whether they were farmers or hunters, Indian people had to share to survive and had learned to maximize their efficiency by following the rhythm of the seasons and moving from place to place as required. As a result, the barter of land for trade goods and, later, money must have had a sense of unreality

about it. Natives may well have been delighted that the Europeans were prepared to pay for the right to use land that Indians regarded as free for anyone's use.

Such optimism, based on an ignorance of European legal concepts, soon turned sour for every people with whom land deals were negotiated. Not only did whites stay put, they also refused to share the land from the moment a treaty or agreement was signed. As far as whites were concerned, if the Indians could not show a legal title to the land, then they would be made to give it up – by force if not by treaty.

Until recently, the outside world generally heard only the white people's view of four centuries of North American history. A case in point is the Battle of the Little Bighorn, otherwise referred to as Custer's Last Stand. The legend is

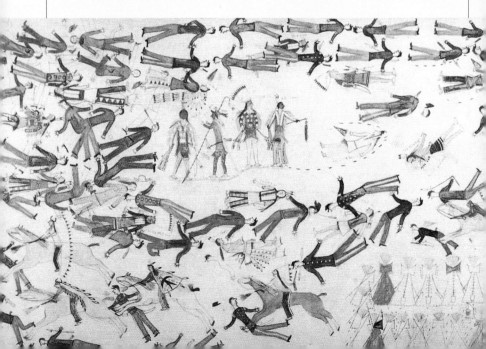

riveting and seductive. On 25 June 1876, a detachment of US Cavalry was ambushed on the Little Bighorn River in Montana and surrounded by Plains Indian warriors. Greatly outnumbered, the soldiers fought gallantly until there was only one man left: General George Armstrong Custer. This Civil War hero, with golden hair down to his shoulders, stood on the crest of a hill, surrounded by the bodies of his men and horses, his guns still blazing, the last man to die. The battle became the most famous event of the Indian Wars, an ignominious defeat transformed into an example of the indomitable pioneer spirit. This version of events was constructed by US army officers, officials, artists and historians. According to the legend, no one had lived to tell the tale of the Last Stand, and in the absence of eyewitnesses white Americans were content to accept the official account.

In fact, many men had survived the battle: Sioux, Arapaho and Cheyenne warriors and their families. Their testimony was ignored because they were Indian and therefore biased – the bias of US officials themselves never coming into question. But accounts retained in Native American oral tradition present a consistent picture of the battle that tallies with the results of recent archaeological work. The Little Bighorn was no heroic, protracted, Last Stand but a disorderly rout, over in half an hour.

The painting by Edgar Paxson (below) shows a buckskin-clad Custer and his troops – including the artist's brother – vainly but valiantly holding off the Indians at the Little Bighorn. The Sioux drawing (below, left) depicts the battle as the chaotic rout it really was. However, Paxson is more truthful in one respect: Custer had had his celebrated long hair cut shortly before the battle.

Leading figures

Native traditions recognize no clear distinction between what Western anthropology would define as mythology, legend and history. A discussion of Native North American "leading figures" from an Indian point of view would include mythological characters such as Raven, Glúskap, Kokopelli and others, who were all remembered as real beings who brought great benefits to the people (see pp.120–123).

Confining the discussion of leadership to humans who have upheld Native integrity in the face of white incursion poses its own difficulties. All Native cultures have celebrated the wisdom, strength and courage of elders, chiefs and holy people of recent generations. But because Native history is an oral tradition, the nature of their contribution to Native life is now largely lost,

since their families and communities were wiped out during the European onslaught. There are notable exceptions, such as Black Elk, an Oglala holy man who lived through the triumphs and sorrows of the last days of Plains Indian freedom (see p.133).

The best-remembered Native figures are the resistance leaders who opposed the troops, settlers and politicians of the incoming Europeans and their American successors. The exploits of war chiefs such as Goyathlay (Geronimo), Sitting Bull, Chief Joseph and others were recounted by their descendants, recorded in official documents and covered by white journalists, writers and photographers. This was especially the case during the Indian Wars of the Plains in the late 19th century. However, the first Native leader to become widely

Sitting Bull (1831–90), more than any other Plains Indian, symbolizes the Indian virtues of generosity, bravery, tenacity and resistance to white incursion. At the age of 10 he proved his generosity by killing a buffalo calf and giving the meat to the needy. By 14, he had counted his first coup on an enemy, showing his bravery. He earned membership in the Strong Heart Warrior Society and was recognized as a wichasa wakan, *or holy man. From 1863, he resisted white intrusion into Hunkpapa Sioux hunting grounds, and he was named principal chief of the Teton Sioux Nation in 1867. In 1876, Sitting Bull had a Sun Dance vision of a victory over white soldiers. A few weeks later, he helped lead Lakota and Cheyenne forces that annihilated Custer's forces at the Little Bighorn River (see pp.30–31). He led his people to Canada, but returned and toured for a time with Buffalo Bill's Wild West Show before retiring to a reservation. In 1890, he was shot dead by tribal policemen who were sent to arrest him for his involvement in the Ghost Dance (see pp.136–7).*

known to outsiders was Wahunson-acock, or Powhatan, chief of the Pow-hatan tribe in the early 17th century. He forged an alliance of southeastern coastal tribes and sought to maintain the integrity of his nation after the English established a colony in Virginia in 1607. A skilled diplomat, Powhatan even allowed his daughter, Pocahontas, to marry an Englishman, John Rolfe. (Rolfe took her to England, where she died of smallpox in 1617, aged 21.)

Native leaders generally found that diplomacy, even when conducted according to Western standards, was to no avail in countering European intrusion. John Ross, the principal chief of the Cherokee nation in the 1830s, did much to "civilize" his people in the eyes of white Americans, only to find them ordered to leave their traditional lands under the notorious Indian Removal Act of 1830. Ross successfully fought the order in the Supreme Court, but the ruling was ignored and he was in the last group to be forced west in 1838. In the following years he worked hard to restore the fortunes of the Cherokee in their new homeland.

Many other leaders, driven by the sheer despair of losing their families and homelands, resorted to armed resistance. In 1763, the Ottawa chief Pontiac, a great orator, joined with a powerful visionary known as the Delaware Prophet to lead northeastern tribes, including the Ojibway, Huron, Seneca and Delaware, against the British. Forts and trading posts fell, almost 2,000 settlers died, and Pontiac and his forces laid siege to Fort Detroit for several months.

In the century or so following the

The name of the Chiricahua Apache chief Geronimo (1829–1909) is synonymous with brilliant military strategy: his resistance to the whites and his phenomenal guerrilla warfare tactics captured the imagination of both Indian and non-Indian alike. Born in southern Arizona, his Apache name was Goyathlay, The One Who Yawns; he was given his Spanish name by the Mexicans after a number of daring raids. He was not a hereditary leader, but often acted as a spokesman for his people. After the Chiricahua were forcibly removed in 1876 to arid land at San Carlos, he and a band fled to Mexico, only to be arrested and returned to the new reservation. In 1881, he resumed his raids, but finally surrendered in late 1886. The army sent him and his followers to Florida and eventually to Fort Sill, Oklahoma, in 1894 (see map on pp.22–3). Geronimo became a rancher. Late in life he appeared at the 1904 Louisiana Purchase Exposition in St Louis, sold Geronimo souvenirs and rode in President Theodore Roosevelt's 1905 inaugural parade in Washington, DC.

foundation of the United States, every tribe had warriors who were willing to fight the US Army, usually against overwhelming odds. Among the more celebrated are the Sauk leader Black Hawk, who led a resistance in the Mississippi Valley in 1832; Manuelito, a Navajo leader between 1863 and 1866; Lone Wolf, a Kiowa chief in the Red River War (1874–5) on the southern Plains; and Dull Knife, a Northern Cheyenne chief, who fought in the central Plains and led a dramatic breakout from captivity at Fort Robinson, Nebraska, in 1879 (see pp.122–3).

The rebellions of these leaders ended in failure, and those who survived had to bear the shame and suffering of defeat. Some, like the Sioux Crazy Horse, remained defiant and died in captivity. Others, such as Geronimo, had their spirits broken or, like Sitting Bull and Chief Joseph, lived out the rest of their days on reservations, often far from their original homelands. To the last, however, they remained preoccupied with the welfare of their peoples. In the case of Sitting Bull, this preoccupation ultimately cost him his life.

The spirit of these resistance leaders persists in the more peaceable, but equally determined, Native leaders of the present day. Activists such as Dennis Banks and Russell Means still press for the right to live in a distinct Native North American society, as do administrators and politicians such as Wilma P. Mankiller, a university-educated activist and former chief of the Cherokee Nation, and Nellie Cornoyea, an Inuvialuk who was elected leader of the government of the Northwest Territories in

Chief Joseph (1840–1904) was a leader of the Nez Perce in Oregon, who at first enjoyed peaceful relations with whites. Joseph, whose father was a Christian convert, initially offered only passive resistance to US government efforts to take away land that had been granted as a reservation in 1855. His people were given just 30 days to relocate to Idaho, and their patience held out no longer. Fighting broke out on 12 June 1877. Successful for three months against superior government forces, Joseph showed great military skill and courage in eluding troops and enemy Indian bands. But the odds turned against him and, a peaceful man at heart, he decided to surrender on 5 October. Joseph is said to have given an eloquent and moving surrender speech including the words: "I will fight no more forever." However, his exact words are not known and were elaborated by journalists. Many of his followers escaped to Canada. Joseph himself was sent to Kansas, then to Indian Territory (Oklahoma). He spent his last days in Washington state, where he died.

1991. These leaders seek compensation for the past loss of lands and people, and aim to secure the educational and economic opportunities that are taken for granted in much of modern North American society.

Native leaders are also gaining more strength through political power in the very assemblies and legislatures that in the past had voted for the removal, con-´finement and destruction of their people. In 1990, Elijah Harper, a Cree member of the Manitoba legislature, single-handedly blocked the passage of the Meech Lake Accord, a proposal to amend Canada's federal constitution in response to demands by the francophone Québecois to be considered a distinct society within Canada. Harper refused to lend support to a bill that did not aim to secure equivalent rights for the country's aboriginal peoples.

In recent years, cultural trends within the dominant white society have tended to heighten the fame of spiritual leaders such as Black Elk. Native North American art has also been brought before an international audience by those who continue to work within Native traditions. Among the more renowned artists are Charles Edenshaw and Bill Reid (see p.119), carvers in traditional Haida style; Charles Loloma, a Hopi jewelry maker; Datsolalee, a Washo basketmaker; and the Inuit sculptors and printmakers Etungat and Kenojuak. In addition, there are many writers, actors, dancers and dramatists whose work, while perhaps adopting Western forms, has also served to show the beauty, drama and colour inherent in aboriginal North American culture.

Born in 1940, the Oglala–Ihanktonwan Sioux Russell Means belongs to the generation of militant Native North Americans who came to prominence in the 1960s. He has courted controversy as a way of showing that Indians remain an important part of North American society in the late 20th century. His career was partly determined by his childhood experience of being moved from a reservation school to California, where he was taunted for being an Indian. He drifted into drugs and delinquency before meeting Dennis Banks, co-founder in 1968 of the American Indian Movement (AIM). Means became a national media figure and led many AIM protests, notably the occupation of Wounded Knee in 1973. He has acted as an attorney in legal cases and has stood for US Vice President. He has also appeared in films, notably The Last of the Mohicans *(1992) and (as the voice of Powhatan) in Disney's* Pocahontas *(1995). Although no longer affiliated with the AIM, Means remains a foremost spokesman for Indian causes.*

Lands and Peoples

The land has always been fundamental to Native identity. Like all peoples, especially in tribal societies, Indians dealt closely with the physical world in every waking moment, whether foraging for plants or stalking game, cutting down a tree, working on the soil, or simply walking through a forest or across a field. The structure of Native life and the nature of Indian cultural expression were determined, above all, by the timeless natural rhythms of the particular environments in which people lived.

The intimacy forged between Indian peoples and the landscape may be strong, but it can rapidly be altered or broken. For example, drought forced the ancient Anasazi to abandon their sophisticated towns and adopt a simpler way of life elsewhere (see p.53). The arrival of horses and guns – both brought by whites – on the Plains and in neighbouring regions created new relationships between hunting peoples and the lands where they hunted (see pp.47–8). However, such changes were more gradual than the traumatic dislocation which occurred as white settlers moved west in the last century, forcing Indian peoples from their traditional landscapes. Despite this, Native life went on, determined as always by what a people could take from the earth and give in return.

In this photograph by Roland Reed (1864–1934), two Navajos look out on the so-called "White House", a ruin set in the face of a huge cliff in Canyon de Chelly, New Mexico. It was built by the Anasazi (see p.53), whose intimate knowledge of the mesas, cliffs and canyons of their homeland is reflected in their skill at constructing villages in the most apparently inhospitable places.

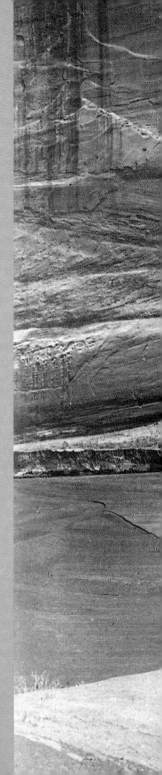

The Northeast

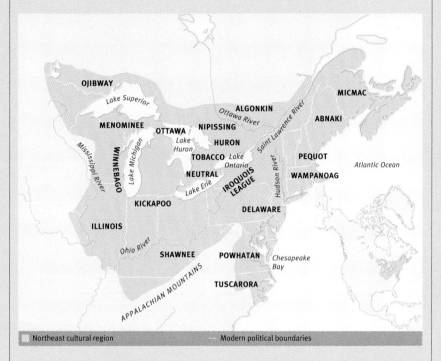

Northeast cultural region — Modern political boundaries

The Northeast is a region of forests, lakes and rivers, stretching from cold, rocky landscapes scoured out by glaciers north of the Great Lakes and the St Lawrence River, to broad, warm and fertile plains along the Atlantic coast and the Mississippi and Ohio valleys.

People on the northern margins of this culture area, bordering the vast pine and spruce forests of the Subarctic, lived with late thaws and sharp, early frosts that would have killed the corn (maize) and other crops grown by their neighbours to the south. So the Ojibway, Abenaki, Micmac and other northern Algonquian-speaking groups led a nomadic life, guiding their birch-bark canoes along seemingly endless lakes and waterways in a seasonal round of hunting, gathering and fishing. The distant ancestors of the more southerly horticultural tribes probably followed a very similar way of life. Campsites left by highly mobile bands of big game hunters have been discovered dating from perhaps as early as 16,000BC, a time when glaciers covered the north.

When Algonquian-speakers travelled through their territory, they often set up simple conical tipis or tents clad with bark or animal skins. At their more permanent summer and winter camps, from which they ranged to gather food, they built wigwams, sophisticated dome structures of saplings covered with sewn birch or elm bark or animal skins.

The people of the northern woodlands gathered a wide variety of plant foods, from wild rice, a seed-bearing grass of lake margins, to blueberries, competing with bears for this delicacy of fire-ravaged hillsides. Animals such as deer and moose were hunted and honoured as gifts of animal spirits (see pp.108–9), who were sometimes recognized as ancestors of the hunters themselves. The Micmac built weirs of stone and interlaced branches to trap eels, and used seagoing canoes to hunt porpoises.

A semi-nomadic life was less necessary south of Lakes Superior and Erie, where a mantle of rich soil covers the bedrock and the hardy spruce and fir are replaced by pine and deciduous forest. Longer summers and milder winters allowed maize, beans and squash to thrive. Algonquian-speakers such as the Illinois, southern Ojibway and Menominee, developed a more settled way of life than their northern neighbours. So too did the Winnebago and other Siouan-speakers, and the Delaware, Wampanoag and other peoples of the Atlantic coastal plain. Hunting and gathering were still important – especially for those who were able to harvest shellfish and other rich resources of the sea – but the agricultural season dominated the rhythm of their lives.

The impact of agriculture is especially seen in the mound-building cultures that developed in fertile river valleys from c.500BC. The Adena were hunters and gatherers, but the resources of the Ohio Valley were so rich that they were able to develop an elaborate ritual and ceremonial life, symbolized by monumental earthworks such as the Great Serpent Mound (see pp.106–7). When the Hopewell culture emerged in the region several hundred years later, its people developed an even more powerful and sophisticated society. Unlike the more or less egalitarian societies around them, the Hopewell seem to have lavished their creative efforts on a social and religious élite. They have left exquisite examples of artistry in stone,

A traditional birch-bark canoe carries an Ojibway family in this photograph taken in Ontario in 1913. The bark of a birch tree was stripped in one piece for the canoes, which were built by specialists.

ceramics, wood and metal, and a grand ceremonial mound complex near the present-day town of Hopewell, Ohio, from which the culture takes its name. The Hopewell eventually transformed the cultural life of the Midwest from the Great Lakes to the Gulf of Mexico for almost 500 years. The Mississippian culture that succeeded the Hopewell *c*.AD700 continued these elaborate traditions (see pp.18–19). But outside the Mississippi valley, northeastern agricultural societies never again conducted their ritual lives on such a scale.

In the inland forests running from Lake Huron eastward and southward to the Appalachian mountains, a distinct group of peoples with their own language, Iroquoian, emerged amid the surrounding Algonquian culture. The Iroquoians were farmers with highly developed slash-and-burn agriculture techniques. In spite of their inferior numbers, they had come to dominate the Northeast by the end of the 17th century. Most Iroquoian-speakers lived south of the St Lawrence River, in what is now upper New York State; another group occupied the lowlands between Lakes Huron, Erie and Ontario. Iroquois life was centred on villages of longhouses, rectangular structures with rounded roofs (see pp.166–7), with accompanying clearings planted mainly with maize. Each longhouse accommodated a number of related families.

THE FUR TRADE

When the French explorer Samuel de Champlain stayed with the Huron in 1615, he saw women grinding corn (maize) to trade with the neighbouring Algonquians for furs and other forest products. De Champlain and other French traders also wanted furs, but not in the small quantities typical of intertribal trade. In return they offered guns, knives, kettles, cloth, liquor and other goods. Some of these items seriously affected native culture, exaggerating the importance of hunting and wiping out traditional manufacture. Alcohol devastated tribal life.

By 1635, the beaver was virtually extinct in Huron territory, but the Huron were able to obtain furs from the Nipissings and Ottawas. The Iroquois were also fur traders and competed with the Huron after their own resources ran out. In 1649, they attacked the Huron and took control of the fur trade.

In the 1840s, the beaver hat went out of style in Europe and the demand for fur plummeted. By this time, however, there were few fur-bearing animals left in northeastern forests.

European fur traders in Canada negotiate the price of a pelt with an Indian trapper in this engraving of 1777.

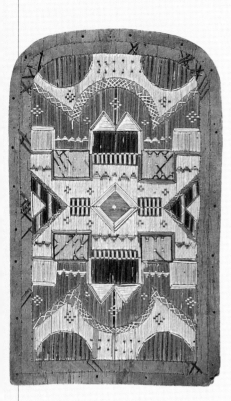

Sometime before the 15th century, five Iroquois groups (the Cayuga, Mohawk, Oneida, Onondaga and Seneca) formed a league or confederacy called the Five Nations of the *Haudenosaunee* ("People of the Longhouse"). The league, which extended from the Hudson River to Lake Erie, was joined by a sixth nation, the Tuscarora, in 1714. During the 18th century, the Six Nations were able to dominate the fur trade. At the height of their power, they controlled the heart of the Northeast, overrunning the Huron to the north and pushing back Algonquians to the east and west. As the foremost Indian power, the league became deeply involved in Anglo-French colonial rivalry. After 1783, they also set an example to the leaders of the new US through their political acumen, diplomacy and command of a vast and complex territory.

A 19th-century chairback made by a Native artesan for the white market. It uses a traditional Northeastern technique of flattened porcupine quills woven in geometric patterns.

LACROSSE

Many Native North American groups play lacrosse, a rough sport with much body contact between two teams occupying opposite ends of a large field (or, in modern times, arena). The word lacrosse comes from *la crosse* ("crosier"), the name given to the game by a French missionary in the 17th century because the players' curved stick reminded him of a bishop's crook. The object of the game is to carry a wooden ball with the stick, which has netting over the end, through the opponent's goalposts, passing the ball as necessary.

Until the early days of European occupation, matches were often played between villages, with teams of up to 100 men each, and many hundreds of spectators. It was, however, more than a game. The Iroquois, to whom we owe the modern form of lacrosse, regarded it as a gift from the Creator. They played it as part of ceremonial occasions, such as planting and harvest rituals, as a way of propitiating spirits.

A traditional Iroquois hickory and rawhide lacrosse stick and large wooden ball.

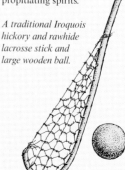

The Peterborough petroglyphs

Near Stony Lake in Peterborough County, Ontario, prehistoric artists carved hundreds of images on a massive outcrop of white, crystalline limestone on the southern fringes of the Canadian Shield. The artists may have been drawn to the site by the strange appearance of the rock. The effects of weathering have left it covered with holes, crevices and hollows that seem to penetrate into the darkness of the underworld. In the spring, the eeriness of the setting is enhanced by noises rising through the holes – the muffled sounds of underground water. Perhaps, to the people who made the pictures, these sounds were considered magical or believed to be the voices of spirits.

Archaeological excavations of soil and debris at the bottom of some of the crevices have revealed fragments of pottery and a number of stone tools. These artefacts suggest that the carvers worked on the site between 500 and 1,000 years ago.

Peterborough is remarkable for the diversity of its images. They range from animal, bird and human figures reminiscent of rock paintings and petroglyphs at other sites in the region, to solar figures and large solar boats that bear a startling resemblance to rock carvings in Scandinavia. The Ojibway call this site *Kinomagewapkong*, meaning "the rocks that teach". For Indians, Peterborough is a place for spiritual reflection and inspiration.

The rock pictures now form part of a Petroglyphs Provincial Park and are protected from further weathering by an aluminium and glass building. The Ojibway are responsible for the care and operation of the site.

PETERBOROUGH

Pacific
Ocean

North
Atlantic
Ocean

Colorado River

Mississippi

Rio Grande

1 The artists of Peterborough pecked out more than 900 human and animal figures, turtles, snakes, canoes and other images in the soft crystalline limestone surface of the rock, using tools of harder stone. Centuries of freezing and thawing have caused further weathering of the crystalline surface, making the originally sharp and clear images almost invisible. In order to record the site, the archaeologists Drs J. M. and R. K. Vastokas darkened the petroglyphs, revealing their beauty and variety to modern viewers. The artists are unknown, but they were probably ancestors of the Algonquian peoples who inhabit the region today, such as the Ojibway. The Algonquians have a rich artistic tradition, as seen in rock paintings scattered across the vast rocky region known as the Canadian Shield, and in the sacred art incised by the Midéwewin on birch bark scrolls.

2 Celestial symbolism is often associated with religious ecstasy, and this large solar figure may represent a holy person, depicted symbolically as one who derives powers from the heavens. According to another theory, it may represent Kitchi Manitou, the Great Spirit of the Algonquians.

3 This boat is unlike any traditional Native vessel. Its bow and stern are elongated and curved upward, and its mast bears a solar symbol. Similar boats incorporating celestial imagery are found only in Scandinavia. This image and the solar figure (2) are among the site's largest petroglyphs, both over three feet (1m) long.

4 For the Algonquians, the turtle is one of the most sacred creatures, as it is a symbol of the earth and its fertility. The oval petroglyphs to the left may represent the creature's eggs.

The Southeast

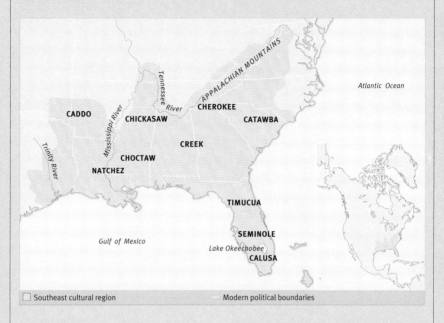

Atlantic Ocean

CADDO

CHICKASAW

CHEROKEE

CATAWBA

CREEK

CHOCTAW

NATCHEZ

Tennessee River

Mississippi River

Trinity River

APPALACHIAN MOUNTAINS

TIMUCUA

SEMINOLE

Gulf of Mexico

Lake Okeechobee

CALUSA

☐ Southeast cultural region   — Modern political boundaries

From the rugged Appalachian mountains to Florida and the Gulf of Mexico and west beyond the lower Mississippi to the arid lowlands of southeast Texas, the warm, wet and fertile Southeast supported a cornucopia of plants and animals. Most of the people living in the region were village-dwelling farmers, but unlike their northern counterparts they could raise two crops of corn (maize) a year, together with squash, pumpkins, gourds and sunflowers. In the subtropical regions, around the Gulf of Mexico, farmers also raised bananas, rice, sweet potatoes and sugar cane. Some tribes, such as the Calusans of southern Florida, remained hunters and gatherers, exploiting the abundant wildfowl, reptiles, fish, whales and seals, and edible roots along the subtropical coastal fringes of the Atlantic and the

Gulf of Mexico. Inland, edible fruits, wild nuts and abundant game were to be found in the region's forests and open country, and the rivers teemed with fish.

Hunting demanded special techniques, because in the Southeast there was no snow to slow down the deer. For example, most southeastern hunters perfected deer calls to attract the animals within the range of their weapons.

Typical dwellings, such as those of the Creeks, consisted of rectangular, gabled mud-plastered summer houses and large, conical winter houses set partly in the ground for insulation. In subtropical areas, housing was open to the hot climate. The Seminoles lived in open-sided dwellings thatched with palm branches.

Because of the great abundance and variety of the plants that grew around them, it is likely that the Indians of the

Southeast had many herbal medicines and used numerous plant substances for ritual occasions. People grew tobacco, which they smoked in pipes during ceremonies and conjuring rituals or rubbed on the body as a healing medium.

When the Spanish arrived in the region at the end of the 15th century, southeastern tribes still bore features of the Mississippian culture, the last of the great river valley civilizations of ancient North America (see p.40). The tribes spoke a diversity of languages: Creeks, Chocktaws and Chickasaws spoke Muskogean dialects, the Catawbas were Siouan-speakers and the Cherokees spoke Iroquoian. It is difficult to obtain a more detailed picture of the region's cultural complexity, since these peoples bore the brunt of early European contacts, beginning with a Spanish expedition in 1513. Successive intrusions of Spanish, French and English colonists and North American settlers brought war, disease and dislocation to the

A 19th-century photograph of a Seminole family outside their palm-thatched hut in Florida. They are wearing traditional long, striped clothing.

THE CHEROKEE SYLLABARY

Cherokee was the first Native language to have its own script, a syllabary created by Sequoyah (1770–1843). He spent over a decade devising his system, which reduced Cherokee to 86 syllables. The script was taken up enthusiastically, and a Bible was published in 1824. A bilingual newspaper, *The Cherokee Phoenix*, and a written Cherokee constitution appeared in 1828. The syllabary undoubtedly helped to preserve Cherokee culture in the face of white oppression in the 1830s and 1840s.

Sequoyah with his syllabary.

Indians and ensured their rapid decline.

The heaviest blow to the southeastern tribes was dealt by President Andrew Jackson, whose Indian Removal Act (1830) forbade Indians to remain east of the Mississippi. The measure was aimed mainly at the peoples who, ironically, had done so much to accommodate the white man that they were known as the Five Civilized Tribes (the Choctaw, Chickasaw, Seminole, Creek and Cherokee). Most were sent west, often on forced marches that left thousands dead (see map, pp.22–3). The Cherokee called their trek "the Trail of Tears", a phrase that other nations adopted to describe their own similar ordeals.

The Plains

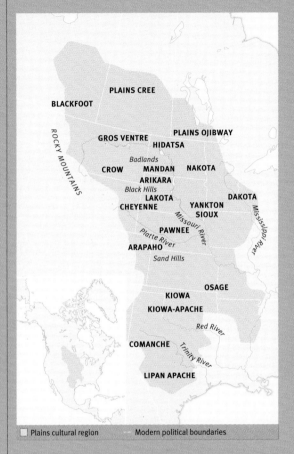

Plains cultural region — Modern political boundaries

The interior of the North American continent consists of vast plains and prairies stretching from the parklands below the ancient granite rock of the Canadian Shield in northern Manitoba, Saskatchewan and Alberta to the lowlands of Texas; and from the crumpled eastern flanks of the Rocky Mountains to the Mississippi Valley. Hills rise up like strange islands in an inland sea: the Black Hills, the South Dakota Badlands, the Sand Hills of Nebraska. River valleys, hidden until the prairie suddenly drops away, provide water, trees, plant and animal life and refuge from biting prairie winds.

Great herds of animals, mainly buffalo (bison), once swarmed beneath the vast expanse of sky, living off the abundant prairie grasses. With no natural barriers in their way and no animal predators, the bison proliferated in their millions. Humans clung to the rivers, initially living off the resources of the valleys, including bear, deer, rabbit and game birds. They hunted bison on foot, trapping them in gullies or driving them over cliffs (see p.48).

Around 1,000 years ago, some groups migrated into the Plains and nomadic groups began to settle in villages, transforming the fertile floodplains into gardens. These cultures thrived until they came into contact with whites. Climatic changes often necessitated adjustments to the village lifestyle when droughts harmed the corn (maize), beans, squash, tobacco and other crops. Villages might also have been forced to relocate because of scarce timber for lodges and fire, or occasional warfare.

Ancestors of the Mandan originated

in the middle Missouri River valley. By the late 12th century, they had come into contact with the ancestors of the Arikara and Pawnee, who migrated from present-day Nebraska and Kansas to escape drought. Some mixing of cultures occurred. By the time the Europeans arrived, most groups lived in large palisaded earthlodge villages along the major rivers. The Pawnee lived in Nebraska, the Arikara in most of present-day South Dakota and the Mandan in North Dakota. These "gardeners" were all highly skilled farmers, whose lives followed a similar rhythm: planting in the spring, buffalo hunting in the summer and early autumn, and harvesting before the long winter.

Life on the Plains was destined to change forever when, in the 16th century, the Spanish reintroduced the horse, an animal extinct in North America for thousands of years (see p.49). First the Pawnee and then, by the end of the 17th century, other tribes in the region adopted the horse and began to range out of the river valleys. Farmers could more easily carry out their seasonal bison hunts. Some woodland tribes, such as the Cheyenne, moved into the Plains to become farmers, but with the horse they rapidly became full-time buffalo hunters instead. With increased mobility and a flood of immigrants into the Plains, further rivalries developed over land and resources.

A critical factor in the adaptation to a more mobile life was the tipi. This conical dwelling, developed by Indians of the northern forests, fitted perfectly into Plains life. The poles and bison skins with which it was constructed could be quickly dismantled and transported by horse-drawn *travois* (see p.49).

By the 19th century, the Plains had become a cosmopolitan landscape. One southern Arapaho chief said that he had met Comanches, Kiowas, Apaches, Caddos, Pawnees, Crows, Gros Ventres, Snakes, Osages, Arikaras and Nez

A woman hanging up meat to dry outside her tipi on the Fort Belknap Reservation, Montana, which is shared by two Plains tribes, the Siouan-speaking Assiniboines and Algonquian-speaking Gros Ventres.

Perces, and communicated with them in the Indian sign language that was once the lingua franca of the Plains.

The introduction of the horse brought many benefits. The gun, however, was a less positive influence. Armed with guns, the northern Algonquians and the Iroquois league (see p.41) expanded westward in their struggle to gain advantage in the fur trade. Under pressure from the east, the Ojibway had pushed the Sioux into the Plains from Minnesota by the early 1700s. The Sioux, in turn, fought for resources with the Mandan, Arikara and Hidatsa along the Missouri River.

Horses made bison easy to hunt, and when breech-loading rifles were introduced in the mid-19th century, the number of buffalo taken by hunters rose dramatically. When whites joined the hunt, the defenceless animal came close to extinction (see p.29), depriving the Plains Indians of one of their greatest natural resources.

White settlement, warfare, disease and the disappearance of the bison spelled the end of traditional Plains Indian life. In due course, peoples who had once freely roamed the great expanses were confined to reservations. There was greater resistance to white encroachment on the Plains than elsewhere, but this ended with the massacre of 200 Lakota Sioux at Wounded Knee in South Dakota in 1890 (see p.137).

THE BUFFALO JUMP

Buffalo have poor eyesight. As grazing animals of the featureless Plains, there was little they needed to see but the grass in front of them. This myopia was a boon to the Indians, especially before they had horses. Hunters would stampede bison toward a cliff or precipice, directing them down a natural gully or creating an artificial channel from rocks and brush. The beasts would not have seen the sudden drop until it was too late, and dozens, perhaps hundreds of animals might die in a single "jump". One site, Head-Smashed-In in Alberta, was evidently used for over 5,000 years to hunt buffalo and contains the bones of hundreds of thousands of animals. The presence of fully articulated skeletons alongside butchered bones shows that sometimes many more animals died than were needed for food, hides and other materials. However, before the animal's decimation in the 19th century, the huge bison population could easily withstand such overkill.

Two hunters in wolfskins approach a herd of buffalo (1822–3), by George Catlin (1794–1872), a celebrated painter of Indian life.

THE HORSE

At first the Indians thought of the horse as a wondrous gift from the spirits. They called the animal "Spirit Dog" or "Medicine Dog" because, as a Spaniard travelling with the gold-hunter Francisco de Coronado wrote in 1541, the Plains Indians traditionally transported their goods from place to place by dog. They used dogs to haul a device that the French called a *travois*, consisting of two long poles with the load suspended between them.

The Plains horse, a short, stocky, shaggy descendant of the mixed Andalusian and Arabian breeds introduced by the Spanish, was a liberating force in the agricultural villages and hunters' camps of the Plains. The new animal brought a fantastic increase in power and mobility, and quickly became indispensable to hunter and warrior alike.

The horse was most often used by men, who were warriors and buffalo hunters, but women in many tribes also owned horses. Horse and rider had to be agile for the buffalo hunt and for competitive intertribal struggles, such as horse raiding, that became a feature of Plains Indian life. People and horses grew together: children rode ponies and quickly learned how to master the equestrian skills that would be essential in adult life. The ability to slip down the side of a galloping horse was an essential skill,

The horses depicted on this 19th-century Sioux beaded waistcoat are ridden by two war chiefs with lances bearing US flags.

because in battle the side of a horse was a vital shield.

Hunters and warriors rode bareback or used small, light saddles stuffed with buffalo hair or grass. For more casual riding, Plains people also made a heavy wooden saddle. They controlled the horse with braided rawhide reins and a bit that was made from a piece of rawhide looped through the lower jaw.

By the beginning of the 19th century, a new and dynamic Plains culture had emerged, one in which the horse was a potent tool, a symbol of status and wealth,

and an expression of tribal pride. The horse was a prestigious possession. Some war chiefs owned herds of more than 1,000 horses, and one Comanche band of 2,000 owned 15,000 horses. A man presented horses to a woman's family when he married her, and horses bore the symbols of the warrior and tribe into battle. Like the battle honours painted on the sides of a modern jet fighter, a horse might bear painted hoofprints to represent previous raids, and handprints to represent enemies killed in combat.

The Great Basin

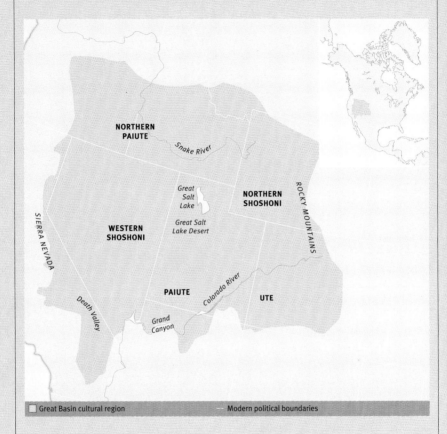

NORTHERN PAIUTE

Snake River

Great Salt Lake

NORTHERN SHOSHONI

ROCKY MOUNTAINS

Great Salt Lake Desert

SIERRA NEVADA

WESTERN SHOSHONI

PAIUTE

Colorado River

UTE

Death Valley

Grand Canyon

☐ Great Basin cultural region — Modern political boundaries

The Great Basin was once a series of huge lakes, hemmed in by mountains and full of the meltwater of ice-age glaciers. But thousands of years of intense summer heat have transformed the ancient lakebeds into rocky desert, and rivers from the surrounding uplands trickle into small, alkaline lakes or simply disappear into the ground.

Survival is not easy in this parched land of sagebrush, pinyon trees and juniper. It favours small game, such as ground squirrels, gophers, rats and jackrabbits, which can burrow or shelter among the rocks and live on seeds, grass and only a little water. Deer and antelope are scarce in the region and keep to the river and lake margins where they can graze and browse. This inhospitable terrain is also the traditional home of hunting and gathering peoples of the Shoshoni, Ute and Paiute nations.

In the more arid parts of the Basin, the people spent most of the year ranging across the desert in small family groups. No one place could yield enough food to support village life, and people had no strong sense of territoriality. Their dwellings were most often simple, open-topped, conical structures made from willow frames covered with brush or reeds. They hunted and gathered what the desert yielded in its seasonal round, from small game, pine nuts and seeds thrashed from grasses, bushes and trees, to ants, grasshoppers, horned toads and lizards.

The Shoshoni and other people of the more arid country had relatively meagre food supplies, but followed the subtle rhythms of the desert to exploit seasonal bounties. In the spring, ground squirrels and groundhogs were still fat and slow after hibernation. Sage grouse were preoccupied during spring mating and could be netted. For those who lived near lakes and streams, fish were available all year round.

As autumn approached, the scattered families began to come together for cooperative harvests of pine nuts. What was not eaten was stored in pits for the winter. The Shoshoni constructed great corrals up to two miles (3.2 km) long of sagebrush, stones and wood, in order to trap antelope, which could not leap over them. Rabbits were flushed from bushes and from the sagebrush into nets. This time of plenty was critical to survival over the winter and also to spiritual well-being. Through ceremony and the sharing of tasks, the people were able to reassert their collective identity and tribal integrity.

There was enough moisture in the region occupied by the Ute to support large game such as elk, bison and mountain sheep, while the Paiute on the eastern Sierra Nevada could irrigate

meadows and maintain their food stocks for longer.

As elsewhere, Europeans had a profound affect on the Basin and its peoples. With the introduction of the horse by c.1700 (see p.47), the Shoshoni in particular turned to the Plains for resources and adopted Plains traditions. When gold was found in California and western Nevada, the people remaining in the Basin could not resist white incursions, as they had nothing to fight with and no warrior tradition. In 1863, the US government simply took over the region. By 1874, most Indians were involved in waged labour or fully dependent on the government.

A late 19th-century photograph of a Ute man by his open-topped willow-and-brush hut in southern Utah. He wears Western clothes: traditionally, Basin peoples wove clothing from shredded sagebrush and cedar bark and, in winter, rabbit skins.

The Southwest

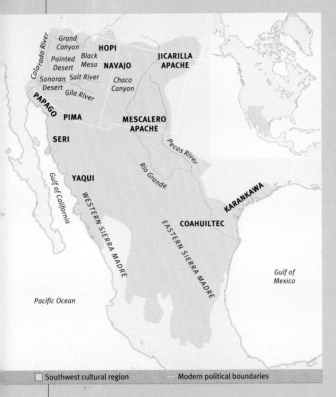

Grand Canyon
Colorado River
Painted Desert
Black Mesa
HOPI
JICARILLA APACHE
NAVAJO
Sonoran Desert
Salt River
Chaco Canyon
Gila River
PAPAGO
PIMA
MESCALERO APACHE
SERI
Pecos River
YAQUI
Rio Grande
KARANKAWA
WESTERN SIERRA MADRE
EASTERN SIERRA MADRE
COAHUILTEC
Gulf of California
Gulf of Mexico
Pacific Ocean

☐ Southwest cultural region   Modern political boundaries

Grande in the east, the Colorado in the west, and the Salt and Gila north of Mexico.

Plants and animals follow a fragile natural cycle, sensitive to variations in moisture. On higher elevations, pine and juniper cluster in shallow soil among the rocks and in the gullies; on the flat desert plains, desert shrubs, cacti and mesquite thrive in all but the driest places, such as Death Valley, which endures extreme heat and endless drought.

Water, or the lack of it, has determined the course of human life in this region. Thousands of years ago, people gathered and hunted as they have always done in deserts, making use of all available living things for food, clothing and shelter. But some of these ancients also raised corn (maize) and squash, using knowledge acquired from Mesoamerica. In the arid Southwest, agriculture flourished to an extent that was rare in North America.

The success of these ancient desert agriculturalists is seen in the elaborate art, technology and ritual of the region's prehistoric civilizations. One group, known as the Mogollon, lived in the mountains, tolerating the extremes of climate in well-insulated pit houses, set three or four feet (0.9–1.2m) into the ground and built with log frames and

The Southwest is an arid, beautiful land of sand and stone, sculpted by millions of years of erosion into flat-topped mesas, dusty plains and deep canyons. Endless shades of red, brown, black and yellow greet the eye, together with the surprising greens of desert plants. Rugged mountains and volcanic domes crowd distant horizons, dark against brilliant deep blue skies. Rain brings life here, most often in short, violent summer storms that briefly flood canyons, stream out over the deserts and quickly sink into the sands. Several large rivers cut through the rocky wastes: the Rio

roofs of sticks, reeds and mud. They grew corn, beans, squash, tobacco and cotton. Their creativity is evident in a type of pottery known as Mimbres, decorated with striking black-and-white geometric designs and figures of animals, humans and other creatures.

Between *c*.AD1200 and *c*.1400, the Mogollon seem to have been overwhelmed by another desert civilization known as the Anasazi ("Ancient Ones"), who first emerged among high mesas and deep canyons *c*.100BC, raising crops on terraced slopes and in irrigated fields. Like the Mogollon, they lived in pit houses, but *c*.AD750, they developed a radical new type of dwelling. It was built of adobe (mud brick) and had a roof of sticks, grass and mud supported by wooden beams.

By joining these houses together, the Anasazi built enormous dwelling complexes or *pueblos* (Spanish: "villages") on mesa tops and in the recesses of canyon walls. Each storey was set back from the one below. One such complex, Pueblo Bonito in Chaco Canyon, was begun *c*.AD900 and has five storeys and around 700 rooms (see pp.56–7).

The Anasazi left behind a wonderful array of painted pots, colourful fabrics, mosaics, exquisite turquoise jewelry, feathered clothing and other elaborate finery. But their civilization was brought to an end by droughts lasting several generations. By *c*.AD1300, the Anasazi had abandoned their settlements and either moved closer to the rivers or reverted to a nomadic hunting and gathering lifestyle.

A view of the terraced adobe dwellings of Taos Pueblo in New Mexico. The home to this day of the Taos people, it is one of a cluster of ancient pueblos around the northern reaches of the Rio Grande.

At the time of the first Spanish incursions in 1539 and 1540, some Indian groups lived in villages and farmed along the rivers or in the desert uplands. These included the Pueblo tribes, Hopi and Zuni, and the Pima and Tohono O'odham (Papago). Others, such as the Apache and Navajo, moved from place to place, hunting and gathering. The Hopi inherited the Anasazi way of life and adapted it to the Colorado River region. At Oraibi Pueblo, perched on Black Mesa in Arizona, Hopi farmers, hunters and gatherers climbed down precipitous tracks cut into cracks and crevices in the sandstone ramparts to the plain hundreds of feet below. Hopi men planted their corn deep in the sandy soil to catch the underground moisture that was fed by summer storms. The women ground the dried kernels into a flour with smooth, hard stones to make *piki*, a flatbread of cornmeal, water and wood ash, baked on a greased slab of sandstone. Women also made wicker baskets of rabbit brush and sumach twigs, and pots in a style reminiscent of the Anasazi, decorated with simple, elegant forms in red, brown and black on the light clay. Men gathered, carded and spun cotton, and women dyed it in the desert colours of yellow, orange, green, black and red, and wove it into cloth.

In the deserts watered by the Salt and Gila rivers, the Pima still follow a way of

CODE TALKERS

In the wars of the 20th century, Native people served in virtually every capacity in the US forces – despite their former hostility to the US military. But Indians viewed service as a way of preserving their proud warrior traditions and tended to be volunteers.

One of their contributions to the US war effort was their ability to communicate in languages of which their enemies had no knowledge. During the First World War, Germans who tapped into Allied lines could not understand the strange words used by Choctaw Code Talkers. In the Second World War, the US Army Signal Corps used men from several Indian nations. Most significantly, the US Marine

Navajo Code Talkers at a 1991 reunion at Window Rock, Arizona.

Corps deployed 420 Navajo men to convey the most important messages among Allied forces in the Pacific. Navajo is spoken by very few people outside the tribe and the Japanese were never able to crack the encoded Navajo communications. The recruits coined new Navajo terms for unfamiliar military concepts. For example, "submarine" was translated into Navajo as "Iron Fish".

life established by another ancient people, the Hohokam. The Hohokam constructed irrigation canals up to ten miles (16km) long in the desert in order to water their fields of corn, beans, squash, tobacco and cotton. In the drier uplands, people such as the Tohono O'odham of the Sonoran Desert harvested cactus – especially saguaro – and hunted small game, including mountain sheep, deer, turkeys, geese and rabbits.

The origins of the Apache and Navajo lie a long way from the Southwest: they speak Athapaskan languages like those of the Indians of the far north of Canada and Alaska. It is uncertain when they migrated south. The Apache generally continued to live the nomadic lives of their northern cousins, hunting bison and antelope on the Plains and deer and elk in the mountains, and gathering wild plants. However, the Jicarilla Apache of northern New Mexico learned agriculture from the Pueblos, although the Apaches did not integrate into the Pueblo cultural landscape. On the contrary, they often fought Pueblos for desert resources. The Navajo retained their ancestral hunter-gatherer lifestyle until they acquired domesticated sheep from the Spanish. They then turned to herding and became expert spinners and weavers. Unlike the restless Apache, the Navajo quickly settled in small, widely scattered groups and adopted the desert as their home.

CACTUS: FOOD FOR BODY AND SOUL

The many species of cactus that grow in the deserts provide both physical and spiritual nourishment. They are a useful source of water in the desert and their juice, flesh or fruit may be used in sacred ceremonies. Beneath the tough skin and dangerous spines, the flesh is moist from the water stored by the plant for the long droughts it must endure. Cactus juice is squeezed out and drunk fresh. The Tohono O'odham (Papago) boil down the sweet juice of the fruit of the saguaro to produce a syrup, which in turn is fermented to make a wine used in an annual rainmaking ceremony. The fruit is also eaten fresh or dried (see also p.112).

Peyote is a spineless cactus that grows mostly underground; above ground there appears only a rounded button which provides a hallucinogenic drug that is used for ritual and non-ritual purposes. Peyote is eaten or drunk in a beverage and is central to the rites of the Native American Church (see p.131).

Tohono O'odham women harvest saguaro fruit with a pole made from dried saguaro ribs.

Chaco Canyon

Chaco Wash, New Mexico, is dry for most of the year, but after thunderstorms it comes to life, carrying torrents of rainwater across the desert. Most of the water eventually disappears into the ground, but where the wash has cut deepest, in Chaco Canyon, the floodplain remains moist enough to support agriculture. In this region, the ancient desert farmers known as the Anasazi (Ancient Ones) established their homeland (see p.53).

The Anasazi began building in earnest in Chaco Canyon from *c*.AD1020 in order to accommodate a thriving farming population. The ruins of nine *pueblos* (villages or towns) are to be found along the canyon, eight in the canyon itself and the ninth, Pueblo Alto ("High Village"), on the north mesa. The surrounding area has yielded thousands of smaller sites of archaeological interest.

Pueblo Bonito ("Beautiful Village"), the largest of the pueblos, became a major processing centre for turquoise. Its skilled workers received the raw material from distant mines and transformed it into polished stones that were traded south into Mexico. The wealth that resulted is suggested by the variety of exotic goods and materials found at Pueblo Bonito, including copper bells, sea shells and parrot feathers.

Anasazi culture came to an abrupt end when the area was hit *c*.AD1130 by a severe drought that lasted for 60 years. Without the seasonal abundance provided by Chaco Wash, the Anasazi could not survive, and by *c*.AD1220 they had abandoned their towns and dispersed to distant river valleys. Chaco Canyon now forms part of Chaco Culture National Historical Park.

Ancient Anasazi roads

Pacific
Ocean

Colorado River

Mississippi

● CHACO CANYON

Rio Grande

North
Atlantic
Ocean

1 *The largest town in Chaco Canyon is known as Pueblo Bonito. It was an architectural marvel. From the outside, it would have appeared like a fortress, encompassed by a massive, almost featureless semicircular wall. However, the wall enclosed a multi-storey complex of nearly 700 rooms facing onto a large plaza – the largest apartment block in the world before the 20th century. The plaza was dominated by two large, circular kivas (ritual chambers), each capable of accommodating hundreds of people. These and nearly 40 smaller kivas attest to the active spiritual life of the pueblo's inhabitants. Some of the first European outsiders to see Pueblo Bonito refused to believe that it was built by ancestors of the present-day Pueblo tribes, and instead attributed it to the Toltec or Aztec civilizations of Mesoamerica.*

2 *A plan of the canyon and its various settlements and other structures, showing the seasonal course of Chaco Wash through the four mesas of the area. The brown lines on the map are long, straight tracks that formed part of a wider network of approximately 400 miles (640km) of roads that held the scattered Anasazi communities together (see also 4, below).*

3 *The Casa Rinconada (see map) is the largest kiva in the canyon. Over 60 feet (18m) in diameter, the kiva had space for up to 250 people. It may have served as a ceremonial centre for several pueblos.*

4 *Some of the "roads" end at the canyon edge, where they lead to flights of carved steps that descend steeply to the mesa floor, as shown here. These roads and steps may have been for ceremonial purposes, rather than for practical, everyday use.*

California

YUROK
HUPA
POMO
Sacramento River
SIERRA NEVADA
COAST RANGES
San Joaquin River
CHUMASH
Mojave Desert
LUISEÑO
Pacific Ocean
Gulf of California

☐ California cultural region
▓ Modern political boundaries

The southwestern edge of North America is enclosed by mountains: a range that follows the coast and runs down into the sea south of Baja California, and the towering Sierra Nevada to the east. The warm Pacific air sheds its moisture in California, watering fertile valleys and transforming parts of the Southwest, Great Basin and Plateau into rocky wasteland and desert. People found the abundance nurtured by this fertile environment irresistible, and settled on rivers, uplands and coastal shores. These ancient migrants came from many other places, as the mixture of languages shows. In general, each of them occupied a small territory that combined uplands and either a river or a stretch of coast. This area contained all they needed to thrive.

On the coast, fish were available most of the year. The Chumash picked shellfish from the sands, and caught tuna, halibut, bonito, albacore and many other fish. They rode the seas in large plank boats, hunting whales, seals, sea lions, dolphins and otters. Inland, deer, rabbits and other small game roamed the landscape, fish swarmed in rivers and streams and the land yielded a cornucopia of wild plants for food and medicine. The autumn acorn harvest was crucial, as it provided a staple food: when acorns are pounded and leached in several changes of water, they make a palatable flour that can be boiled into mush or baked as an unleavened bread.

The Luiseño, who lived north of Baja California, could easily harvest the bounties of land and water in one place, but for most Californians, the seasonal cycle involved a longer journey to and from the sea.

Food resources were so well defined in time and place that the hunting and gathering life followed regular rhythms, more like that of settled agriculturalists than of the foragers of the plains and woodlands to the north and east. A group might make temporary tipi dwellings of redwood bark. When they travelled further into the interior, they might take with them a complete winter village of pole frame and thatch dwellings, each housing several families, and even a ceremonial lodge for communal gatherings.

There was some group control of land that was particularly rich in resources. The Chumash, for example, divided up hunting lands, and other groups owned wild plant tracts, animal habitats and prime fishing spots. In some places, several extended families combined to form larger entities with definite territories, each with a main village and chiefs.

With such plenty, trade was common. The Hupa bartered acorns and other interior foods with the Yurok for seaweed, dried fish and redwood dugouts. Californians used forms of money, such as dentalia shells, in trade, as symbols of power and status, and as burial goods.

Wealth of a different kind was to be the undoing of the first Californians. The discovery of gold in 1848 accom-

Captain John, a leading figure among the Hupa Indians, seen here in 1905 outside a traditional plank hut, part of which is below ground.

plished what Spanish and Mexican missions did not. Floods of settlers came in search of gold and found the riches of the landscape. The Hupa managed to survive, protected in their isolated river valley, but for the Chumash, Luiseño, Pomo and other peoples, the life of plenty came to an abrupt end.

Californian Indians were expert basket-weavers. Pomo women and men wove containers, pots, hats and other articles with colourful geometric designs, sometimes even working in feathers and shells. The impact of the European presence is clearly evident in this Pomo basket decorated with a geometric representation of a train. The basket is made using a traditional Pomo coiling technique.

The Northwest Coast and Plateau

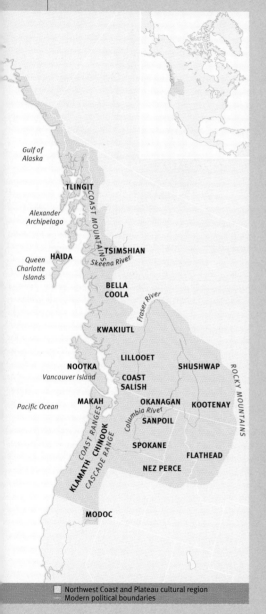

Gulf of
Alaska

TLINGIT

COAST MOUNTAINS

Alexander
Archipelago

HAIDA   TSIMSHIAN
Skeena River

Queen
Charlotte
Islands

BELLA
COOLA

Fraser River

KWAKIUTL

LILLOOET

NOOTKA   SHUSHWAP
Vancouver Island   COAST
SALISH

ROCKY MOUNTAINS

Pacific Ocean

MAKAH   OKANAGAN   KOOTENAY
SANPOIL

COAST RANGES

Columbia River

CHINOOK   SPOKANE

KLAMATH   FLATHEAD
CASCADE RANGE   NEZ PERCE

MODOC

☐ Northwest Coast and Plateau cultural region
— Modern political boundaries

The western mountains sweep down to the sea along the Northwest Coast. Where there are no large offshore islands to offer protection, the Pacific surf crashes against steep and densely wooded slopes and the tides surge many miles up steep flooded valleys into cool inland forests. Warm ocean currents weave among the islands and along the coastal plains, creating lush temperate rainforests fringed by sand and smooth rock beaches. Beyond the coastal mountains and fjords is a large dry plateau where coniferous forests are broken by a hilly terrain of open grassland and sagebrush, dotted with oak. Glacier meltwater from surrounding mountains feeds scattered lakes and two great river systems, the Columbia and the Fraser.

The peoples of these contrasting landscapes shared a reliance on the salmon. In the spring, mature adult fish swarmed far upstream from the sea to spawn in shallow river gravels. Salmon was a food source as predictable as the seasons, and the only agriculture in the fertile river deltas and on the coasts was some scattered tobacco growing.

Even without salmon, food on the coast was abundant: trout, cod, halibut, herring, smelt and other fish. One small fish, the oolichan, contained so much oil that it could be dried, run through with a wick and burned like a candle. Sea mammals also flourished. The Nootka and Makah hunted whales, and all peoples took seals, porpoises, sea lions and sea otters. Clams, mussels, sea urchins and oysters were so plentiful that ancient village sites are marked by heaps of shells many feet deep. Surrounding woods were full of starchy roots and berries, as well as deer,

The Kwakiutl village of Newitti on Vancouver Island, 1881. The cedar houses, totem pole and canoes are typical of this part of the Northwest Coast. The elaborate decoration of the house on the right indicates its owner's status: it was home, the sign in English declares, to Newitti's "head chief".

beavers, bears, marten and other small game. Hunters at higher altitudes could pursue elk, goat, wolf and grizzly bear.

This great natural abundance nurtured a culture that became as elaborate as any in North America. Its raw material was the soft but durable red cedar (see p.63). Northern houses had log uprights sheathed in overlapping cedar planks, with a large ridgepole holding up a gabled roof. The houses were often carved and painted. Houses in the south of the region were bigger, but had shed roofs and little or no decoration. A number of related families shared the windowless interior, each family occupying a shelf-like space around a large, communal central area.

Northern artists carved and painted poles, house fronts, boats and even household utensils with heraldic crests in amazingly intricate and distinctive styles. So-called "totem poles" were the most vigorous artistic expression of a belief in fundamental creative forces, especially among the Tlingit, Haida and Tsimshian. This artistic energy went hand in hand with the highly class-conscious nature of much of Northwest Coast society. In those parts of the region where people were classed as nobles, commoners or slaves, the material representation of status was essential. Individuals, families and clans owned and displayed images of animal ancestors and other mythological figures. They held the rights to names, titles, songs, dances and myths, as well as to fishing and hunting grounds and shellfish beds. In areas where society was less stratified, as among the Salish and Chinook, there were fewer status symbols, and artists confined their work mainly to religious objects.

Inland, people living on the Fraser and Columbia river systems were hunters and gatherers, relying on fish, deer, elk, mountain sheep, rabbits and other small game, and on grassland and forest plants. However, they were not entirely isolated from the cultures around them. Pacific Coast culture had been brought to them in trading canoes probably since ancient times, as suggested by stone carvings of human and animal effigies. In more recent times, groups such as the Nez Perce found that the horse was ideally suited to the grasslands of the Plateau, and consequently emulated the lifestyles of the Plains.

THE POTLATCH

In communities where each individual had a defined rank and status, people would demonstrate the extent of their material wealth by giving part of it away – or even burning it – at a potlatch ceremony. A clan chief or other noble would entertain sometimes hundreds of guests with spectacular dances and huge feasts. The wealth involved was truly impressive: goods given away or piled up in bonfires might include cloth, furs, clothing, basketry, utensils, beads and canoes.

The potlatch was traditionally held to mark rites of passage such as birth, puberty, marriage, inheritance and death. At a potlatch, a clan would display its wealth, strength and continuity with the past. Each song, dance, image and costume represented the

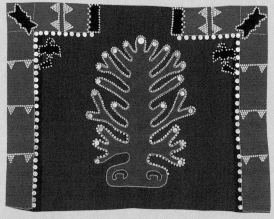

A Kwakiutl blanket of c.1900 with mother-of-pearl button design. Such blankets were worn at potlatches and other special occasions.

clan's inheritance and vitality.

Potlatching reached great heights with the arrival of cheap mass-produced European trade goods: on one occasion, 33,000 blankets were given away. When traditional life came under

pressure, potlatches took on such huge proportions that the Canadian government banned them in 1885 as wasteful and anti-progressive. However, they continued in secret in many places before the ban was lifted in 1950.

THE CEDAR TREE

The lush, dense rainforests that cover the islands and mountain slopes along the Pacific Coast were once dominated by red cedar trees. Unlike the straight and sober Douglas fir and the gnarled arbutus, the mature red cedar was a shaggy giant, its massive ribbed and lined trunk rising high out of the dense undergrowth. Shredded cedar bark was a valuable source of fibre that was woven into a wide range of objects, such as baskets, ropes, mats, capes and various other forms of clothing.

Cedarwood itself is soft and easily worked, but also highly resilient, resistant to the wet climate and salty sea air. Elaborately carved cedar totem poles survived longer than the villages in which they stood. Large cedar logs were sometimes dug out, widened in the middle by a process of steaming and stretching, and chiselled to produce streamlined, ocean-going canoes – those of the Haida could be up to 70 feet (21m) long. Carvers transformed wooden blocks into dramatic masks and elaborate feast bowls, and they reproduced the dense and complicated styles of Northwest Coast painting on wooden panels.

The grain of cedar is so straight that the wood can easily be split into long, thin planks and shingles, ideal for the construction of the large communal houses typical of the Northwest Coast. The softness and straightness of the wood were also exploited to make "bentwood" boxes, which were steamed and bent into shape from a single plank of cedar.

A Nootka shrine in its original location at Friendly Cove, Vancouver Island. At the shrine, an important individual underwent ritual purification in order to encourage whales to beach nearby to provide the people with food and other resources. In 1904, the shrine, with its 80 cedarwood guardian effigies (left), was dismantled and shipped away to the American Museum of Natural History.

The Subarctic

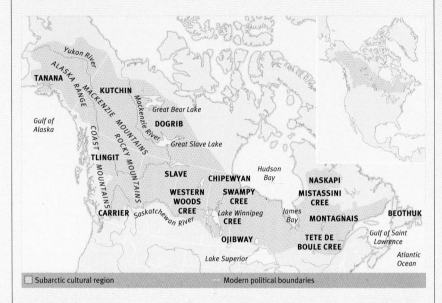

Yukon River
ALASKA RANGE
TANANA
KUTCHIN
Mackenzie River
Great Bear Lake
Gulf of Alaska
MACKENZIE MOUNTAINS
DOGRIB
ROCKY MOUNTAINS
Great Slave Lake
COAST MOUNTAINS
TLINGIT
Hudson Bay
SLAVE
CHIPEWYAN
NASKAPI
WESTERN WOODS CREE
SWAMPY CREE
MISTASSINI CREE
CARRIER
Saskatchewan River
Lake Winnipeg
CREE
James Bay
MONTAGNAIS
BEOTHUK
OJIBWAY
TETE DE BOULE CREE
Gulf of Saint Lawrence
Lake Superior
Atlantic Ocean

☐ Subarctic cultural region   —— Modern political boundaries

North of the prairies and the woodlands of the Northeast, and sweeping around Hudson Bay, is an immense forest, interrupted by innumerable lakes, bogs, streams and rivers. Hardy pine, spruce and fir thrive on thin, rocky and infertile soils; and in sheltered spots, aspen, willow and birch tolerate the long and extremely cold winters. Lichens and mosses are everywhere, clinging to trees, rocks and the ground. Further north, the forest gives way to a frigid tundra. Subarctic summers can be warm, but in the tundra and the adjacent forests this is not a time of ease, because the air is clogged with blackflies, mosquitoes and other biting insects. Under a thin mantle thawed by the sun, the ground remains permanently frozen.

Most people in this rugged land hunted, fished and foraged in small,

family bands. East of the Rockies, the Chipewyan, Dogrib, Slave, Kutchin (Gwich'in) and others spoke Athapaskan languages. The glacier-scoured granite landscape around Hudson Bay and eastward to the Atlantic Ocean was home to Algonquian-speakers, including the Cree, Ojibway, Naskapi and Montagnais peoples.

Hunting groups all followed the game. In the winter, they lived by frozen lakes to ensure a supply of fish, setting up lean-tos or small tipis. But they also moved about, either on foot with snowshoes or by sled and toboggan. Some groups recognized family hunting and trapping territories, and all returned year after year to favoured hunting, fishing or gathering spots. It was easy to pursue caribou, moose and other game that left tracks in the snow. When the spring thaw turned the land into bog, the people kept to the rivers and lakes in birch-bark canoes.

Life in the northern Subarctic revolved around the caribou, or reindeer. People used all parts of the animal for a range of purposes, from caribou-hide tipi covers to weapons and tools made from bone and antler. Caribou spend the winter in small scattered groups inside the tree-line, but early in the spring they migrate to calving grounds far north in the tundra. In the brief northern summer, they trek back south with their calves. En route, they are harassed by wolves and, at river crossings, where they are most vulnerable, by people.

Other game included moose, musk ox, deer, fur-bearing animals such as beaver, mink, hare and otter, and, in the forests north of the Plains, bison. The western mountains of the Yukon and Alaska had Dall sheep and mountain goats. Throughout the forests, porcupines provided meat, as well as quills, which were dyed, flattened and embroidered into clothing and accessories. Wildfowl were plentiful. Plant foods were most common in the southern forests – berries, roots, wild rice and the soft inner bark of poplar.

Farther north, the Chipewyan lived almost entirely on meat and fish. Isolation and hardship did not prevent these northern bands from maintaining networks of relations over great distances, exchanging marriage partners, gathering for caribou hunts or making contacts through trade in the copper, flint and quartzite needed for tools.

Two Kutchin (Gwich'in) women photographed in 1982 outside their winter hunting lodge in the Yukon. Subarctic women are skilled at trapping small game. They are also traditionally responsible for skinning caribou and tanning its hide, as well as for butchering and preparing the meat.

The Arctic

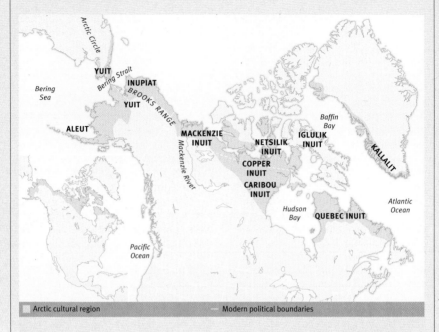

YUIT
Bering Strait
INUPIAT
Bering Sea
BROOKS RANGE
YUIT
Arctic Circle
ALEUT
MACKENZIE INUIT
Mackenzie River
Baffin Bay
NETSILIK INUIT
IGLULIK INUIT
KALLALIT
COPPER INUIT
CARIBOU INUIT
Hudson Bay
QUEBEC INUIT
Atlantic Ocean
Pacific Ocean

☐ Arctic cultural region　　　　　— Modern political boundaries

The land near the top of the world is a vast frigid waste stretching from Siberia to Greenland, its shores bounded by the Pacific, Arctic and Atlantic oceans. For three months in the summer people live in endless sunshine, but in winter the sun slips below the horizon for three months of perpetual night, lit only by the moon and stars, the northern lights and the glimmer of twilight in the south.

In winter, this seems like the harshest land on earth. The temperature remains below freezing for up to nine months, transforming both land and sea into an indistinguishable expanse of craggy ice and wind-whipped snow. But as the land warms in the rising sun, the snow melts to reveal a treeless, stony tundra covered with lichens and mosses, hardy flowering plants and grasses, and small patches of dwarf willow and other scrub. Sea ice retreats from the mainland coast and southern offshore islands. Animal life emerges: seals climb onto ice floes to bask in the sun, walruses gather along the shore, herds of caribou return to calve and musk oxen browse new growth on the bushes. The air is full of the sounds of birds: ravens, ptarmigan and snowy owls, which have wintered here; and other species returning to breed after a winter in the tropics. Grizzly bears, wolves, foxes and weasels prowl for ground squirrels, lemmings and other small game.

People began to hunt and fish along the Arctic coasts c.4,500 years ago, drawn from the Pacific Coast by the animal wealth. The first peoples in the central and eastern Arctic are known to anthropologists as the Dorset and the Thule. They had kayaks, sleds and other equipment essential to life in the snow. The Thule hunted whale and other sea mammals. Several hundred years ago, the climate cooled and only the sea adjacent to the warm Pacific currents remained open. Those people remaining in the central and eastern Arctic became seal hunters.

The present-day Arctic peoples – the Inuit and the Aleut – are closely related, speaking languages of one family, Eskimo-Aleut. They are different in physical appearance from other Native North Americans, closely resembling the peoples of the far northeast of Asia. The Aleut live on the Aleutians, a chain of nearly 100 barren islands strung out between Asia and North America. They resemble the Inuit physically, and like them they hunt sea mammals. The Aleut and Inuit have traditionally shared some of the same technology: both used kayaks, burned seal oil in stone lamps and lived in large communal houses set partly underground and roofed with driftwood or whalebone and sod.

However, the Pacific gave the Aleut a different way of life. They fished for salmon, gathered shellfish and sea urchins, caught octopuses among the rocks, dug up edible roots and picked berries. The Aleut had extensive contacts with the Tlingit and other peoples of the Northwest Coast region to the south. Aleut society, like that of its southern neighbours, was highly stratified, with the people classed as chiefs,

An Inuit dog team pulling a sled on the frozen sea near Iglulik, north of the Arctic Circle on the Melville Peninsula. Before the advent of the horse, dogs provided the main mode of transport for many of the aboriginal peoples of North America (see also p.49).

An Inuit hunter dressed in a polar bear pelt, part of the traditional method of training hunting dogs to recognize the scent of their prey.

commoners or slaves. The Aleuts also recognized the material wealth that this stratification required.

The Inuit live from sea to sea across the extent of the north polar cap. All Inuit peoples, from the Yuit of Siberia to the Kallaalit of Greenland, share both language and lifestyle. The Inuit of the vast region from the Mackenzie River to Hudson Bay, including the Netsilik, Iglulik and Aivilik, led the life that the rest of the world identifies as "Eskimo", although the Inuit dislike this name (see p.10). To resist the cold they wore thick parkas, trousers of caribou hide (with the hair against the skin) or polar bear skin (with the fur outside), and boots of caribou or sealskin. Like their ancient ancestors, they used dogsleds and built temporary snow houses (igloos) when travelling in the winter. Their equipment included snow goggles that were worn against the blinding reflection of sun on snow and ice in the spring and summer.

The Inuit year was organized around hunting. In the winter, a number of families would gather together to hunt seals, the main source of food. Seals must breathe several times an hour, so as the water begins to freeze they keep small breathing holes open by scratching the ice away from beneath. Dogs helped the Inuit to locate these holes, which were often hidden under drifting snow, and hunters might then have to wait many hours in the cold before they could spear their prey. When a sealing ground was exhausted, the people moved camp.

As soon as the snow melted on the tundra, the large winter camps broke up, and the Inuit ranged across the tundra in small family groups to take advantage of the brief, intense explosion of life in the spring and summer. They trapped fox and other small game, fished for cod in the sea, set up weirs for char and other fish in the rivers, hunted birds and gathered eggs. Seals were easier prey as they sunned themselves on ice floes in the open water and gathered in their breeding and feeding grounds. Beluga whales appeared, sometimes in great numbers. The walrus hunt was important, because walrus ivory was essential for tools and weapons. It was also an ideal medium for carving small, intricate human, animal and spirit figures – an artistic tradition going back to ancient times. Some Inuit headed south to hunt caribou at their river crossings.

By August, the first persistent snows had arrived, and by September, rivers and lakes were frozen. The small family groups returned to the coast to await the ice, the seals and the long winter.

WHALING

Whaling is a dangerous task: hunters must venture into the open sea and manoeuvre among a herd just to harpoon one creature. But the effort is worthwhile, because many families can be provided for by the tons of meat and blubber yielded by one whale.

The whaling season begins in spring, when bowhead whales migrate north along the coasts of Alaska and Labrador to their summer haunts near the polar icecap. Whale hunters take to the sea in a *umiak*, a boat of driftwood covered in stretched walrus hide or sealskin. It is about 30 feet (9m) long and can hold a crew of up to ten. When a whale surfaces near the boat, the harpooner plunges his weapon,

Inuit walrus-ivory charms are used to lure fish and whales.

once tipped with ivory but later of steel, into the animal. The wounded whale dives quickly, pulling with it a line to which inflated floats made of sealskin are attached. Each time the struggling animal comes to the surface, the hunters spear it with more harpoons. Finally, exhausted from its injuries and its attempts to dive while restrained by the floats, the whale gives up the fight and is despatched with one last thrust of a hunter's lance.

The hunters tow the dead whale to shore – a difficult task in heavy seas – where the animal is butchered. Its flesh and blubber are shared among the people and surplus meat is stored in "larders" dug into the permafrost. Whale blubber is rendered into oil for trade

Patterns and symbols

People of all Native North American cultures use art to express their connection with the sacred earth and the plants and animals with which they share it. The symbols and patterns on everything from pots to footwear allow artist and people to reflect on the world around them and to be reminded of its religious and secular significance. Finely-made objects are also intended to be enjoyed in themselves, and artistic skill is traditionally highly prized. As in other cultures, access to the best artists and craftspeople was a mark of social prestige among Indian peoples.

Decorative patterns and symbols can be made from, and applied to, almost any material. Hides may be painted or covered with beads or quills. Wood, antler, bone, shell and stone are carved, etched or painted. Clay pottery or figures are also often incised or painted. Plant fibres and animal hair are spun and woven into netting and textiles.

Motifs are to some degree limited by the medium. Baskets, beadwork and woven fabrics commonly have geometric patterns, which are the easiest to execute in these media. Where naturalistic figures are used, the limits of the material may result in a degree of stylization. Greater naturalism may be found in painting and carving, but truth to nature is not necessarily an artistic or

ABOVE *In this photograph of c.1900, a Haida woman paints a woven hat with characteristic motifs. Male and female artists might specialize – for example, on the Northwest Coast, basketweaving was* more often done by women, who used a range of techniques to make baskets, cradles and even watertight cooking vessels from bark fibres and grasses. They were particularly skilled at fine work with spruce roots.

ABOVE *Butterflies of many colours adorn this basket made in traditional style by Paiute craftswoman Marilu Lehi in 1984.*

cultural ideal. Individual artists work inside established traditions, but may experiment within acceptable limits.

Symbols and patterns often reflect the artist's natural surroundings. For example, woodlands art often uses floral and other plant motifs, while coastal groups tend to depict sea animals. Other motifs are drawn from the people's cosmology, and mythical creatures such as thunderbirds, serpents and other supernatural beings are frequently encountered.

A number of regions are renowned for their skilled basketmakers – for example, the Southwest and the Northwest Coast. Among the Hopi, utilitarian and ceremonial basketry most often displays geometric, animal and *kachina* spirit designs. Triangles and concentric circles are the most popular geometric motifs, which frequently include bright colours and intricate patterns. The eagle and the Crow Mother Kachina are common subjects, but turtles have recently become more popular. Basketweavers of the Northwest Coast draw upon a range of animal and anthropomorphic motifs (see pictures below and on opposite page).

Pueblo potters are also celebrated for the elegance and intricacy of their work, which continues a tradition with roots in the great pre-contact cultures of the region, such as that of the Anasazi.

TOP *Stylized motifs from the Southwest representing real and mythical animals. Left to right: Cloud Serpent, deer, lion, turtle, Rain Serpent.* ABOVE *A* kachina *motif from a Hopi basketwork tray.*

ABOVE *A killer-whale hunt is depicted among the designs on this 18th-century Nootka woman's woven hat. The killer whale, or orca, is often denoted by its prominent dorsal fin.*

ABOVE *Northeast woodlands art often uses motifs reflecting the region's rich vegetation. The Ojibway design (top) is geometric and stylized, in contrast to the Menominee floral pattern (bottom).*

Geometric and traditional animal motifs, such as serpents and thunderbirds, are depicted in black, white and rich natural reds, browns and creams.

More than 30,000 Navajo women are weavers, and their rugs show an astonishing variety. According to Navajo legend, the weavers learned their craft from Spider Woman, a being who instructed them how to weave grass, yucca, cedar bark and cotton. However, as the Navajo became shepherds, wool came to be the dominant material. The colours used in Navajo rugs have changed in recent times from natural earth hues to pastels for the tourist market. There are several regional styles of patterning.

For example, the "crystal" style basically uses stripes, with many variations. *Yei* ("god") and *Yeibichai* ("masked dancer") rugs employ motifs from sacred sandpaintings, although the rugs have no ritual significance of their own.

Around the Great Lakes, skilled workers flatten porcupine quills and dye them with plant pigments. The quills are then used to decorate bags and moccasins. Women of the Huron, Micmac and other Northeastern tribes embroidered skins, cloth and birch bark with dyed moose-hair. As colourful glass beads were traded into the area by Europeans, they were combined with traditional materials or even replaced

TOP *A range of moccasin designs from the Great Plains (Dakota, Blackfoot and Arapaho). Geometric designs based on circles, chequered patterns and zig-zags predominate.*

ABOVE, LEFT *In many Native traditions, the sky and its powers, such as rain, thunder and wind, are embodied by the Thunderbird, a giant eagle. This stylized Thunderbird is from an ancient Pueblo pot.*

ABOVE *A blanket or shawl made by an Osage weaver of the southern Plains. Red was considered the colour of life, and was often used in garments for women, who were revered as the givers of life.*

them altogether. Intricate floral motifs are most common, but simple geometric patterns may adorn a utilitarian object such as a knife sheath or pouch.

The people of the Plains also used quillwork for their pipebags and moccasins. Bison-hide tipi covers and individual hides may bear naturalistic images of buffalo or horses, but otherwise, Plains patterning tends to be more geometric, with circles, rectangles and triangles. Circles may symbolize the dome of the sky, a domed earthlodge or the floor of a tipi. As in many other Native North American cultures, the circle was an expression of the relatedness of everything on the earth and of the eternal cycles of nature.

Much art of the Northwest Coast is described as representational – that is, key elements or characteristics of an animal or person may be emphasized, sometimes to the exclusion of any other feature. For example, a beaver may be represented only by two large front incisors and a broad, cross-hatched tail, and ravens and seahawks by their characteristic beak and eyes. In the three-dimensional carvings on totem poles, the representation might be more complete than on two-dimensional objects. Animal figures are often anthropomorphized, combining both animal and human features.

ABOVE *A late 19th-century Navajo "steer weaving" blanket, showing two steers against a striped background, with chequered diamond motifs around the edges. The stripes are arranged in five bands, a typical Navajo design of this period. The head between the two animals resembles the sacred figures in Navajo sandpaintings and may represent a Yei (god) or some other sacred being.*

ABOVE *Anthropomorphic animal figures from Haida totem poles. Clockwise from top left: a hawk (curved beak), raven (straight beak), bear (long tongue) and beaver (large incisors and broad tail).*

The Life of the Spirit

According to Native North American traditions, everything that the Creator made, whether animate or not, has a spirit. Therefore, all things are related and all things are sacred. Relationships between humans, Mother Earth, other creatures and the ancestors are well defined. The earth provides for the "two-leggeds" – the people – and for all others who were put on it by the Creator. People are therefore expected to respect the earth. Many "four-leggeds" – the animals – willingly sacrifice themselves to feed and clothe the people, who in consequence are obliged to show respect for them. The ancestors, who dwell in the realms of the spirits, gave life to those who now live, and the living, for their part, must respect the ancestors. Humans must also respect their living kin, and must provide and care for each other in order to survive.

This complex system of mutual respect is expressed not only in daily life, but also in the people's ritual and ceremonial practices. Every traditional rite and ceremony celebrates the spirit that unites all things on earth and reaffirms the sacred relationships.

An Indian dancer at a powwow (see pp.90–91). Dance is central to much Native American ceremonial. The most colourful dance costumes are for "fancy dancing"; more traditional costumes employ more natural colours, furs and fewer feathers.

Foundations of the sacred

It is not entirely appropriate to speak of Native North American "religions" or "belief systems", since these terms often imply a formally-structured spiritual life conducted alongside, but distinct from, everyday secular existence. However, in Native North American societies the threads of ordinary life and spirituality are so tightly interwoven that the sacred and the secular are indistinguishable. Indian sacred life extends beyond the communal festivals and ceremonies that punctuate the year and the rituals that accompany puberty and

Prehistoric rock art at Harvest Scene Site in Utah depicts elongated figures which are thought to be sacred beings. These petroglyphs, which are perhaps 2,000 years old, may have been produced as part of propitiation rituals.

other times of passage (see pp.100–103). For many Indians, the simplest everyday act has spiritual meaning.

The sacred life of each Indian nation is unique and intimately linked to its own particular environment. It is based on the sense of community that a people develops with the local landscape and climate, and with the beings and spirits that are perceived to dwell around them. However, Native traditions do share certain common underlying concepts and attitudes. Spirit power – "medicine" – is believed to reside in all things. Every plant and animal, even the soil itself, possesses a soul that is mutually dependent on other souls. The cycles of nature, such as the seasons and the passage of the sun and moon across the sky, are evidence of the eternal circle of existence and the timelessness of Creation.

Some peoples view the powers that maintain the world as entities revealing themselves in the form of natural phenomena, such as winds, rivers, corn (maize) and buffalo. These are regarded as relatives, and community life is structured around the rights and obligations due to such kin. For other peoples, the controlling powers are formless, mystic energies, such as the Manitou of the Algonquians, Wakan of the Lakota and Sila of the Baffin Bay Inuit.

Each Native people has its own ways of conducting its relationship with the cosmic entities, of controlling and harnessing the "medicine". Some individuals actively seek the power to deal directly with the spirits; others acquire it by accident of birth or through a life crisis. However, everyone must pay due heed to the spirits every day as part of his or her obligations to them just for being alive. The notions of good or evil are expressed largely in terms of whether or not obligations to the spirits are being met. Failure in this regard is a sign of disrespect, and upsets the balance and harmony of the world. Most virtues taught by elders, such as wisdom, bravery, generosity and selflessness, aim to ensure proper respect, so that the cosmic balance may be maintained or restored and the community's survival guaranteed.

MEDICINE WHEELS

Scattered across the plains and prairies of North America are large stone circles known as "medicine wheels". They were built out of the small boulders left on the surface of the earth by retreating glaciers. The "hub" of each medicine wheel is a pile of stones, or cairn; other cairns may be positioned around the circumference. Lines of stones sometimes radiate like spokes from the central cairn to the outer ring.

The best-known of these structures is the Big Horn medicine wheel in Wyoming, which is nearly 100 feet (30m) in diameter with 28 spokes and six small cairns around the rim. The identity of its builders, and when and why it was made, are unknown. A widely-held theory is that the "spokes" of

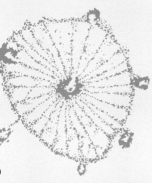

a medicine wheel are (or were originally) aligned with astronomical events, such as the position of the sun at dawn on Midsummer's Day.

Another theory is that medicine wheels are more purely symbolic, perhaps intended as visual representations of sacred cyclical principles that bind the universe. They resemble forms found in Native dance and the shape of some lodges. Many are on high ground, so their form may symbolize the dome of the heavens.

A plan of the Big Horn wheel. The hub and protruding cairn align with the rising sun on the summer solstice.

The medicine wheel in the Big Horn mountains of northern Wyoming. It may have been constructed by one of the Plains peoples, such as the Arapaho, Cheyenne or Crow.

Nature and spirit

According to many Native North American traditions, nature and spirit are inseparable and mutually dependent: spirit resides in all things and all things are part of nature. The earth is at the centre of this scheme. Most Native peoples respect the earth as the source of an endless cycle of generation, destruction and regeneration, through which all things are believed to pass. The view of the earth as a powerful nurturing force is expressed in the common Native concept of Mother Earth, but there is considerable scholarly controversy as to whether this imagery predates contact with whites or is essentially a European construct.

Fundamental to many Native narratives is the understanding that the earth acts as a host to human beings. Many Native traditions view humans as spiritually rooted in the earth, which gave them life just as the soil gives life to a plant. But people are seen as no more important than any other living or non-living thing. All beings must share the earth as equal partners, each responsible to the other.

This attitude is in contrast to that of the Judaeo-Christian tradition brought by missionaries, in which God gave humans dominion over the earth and all other creatures. Animals are widely revered in Native North American traditions, and some peoples believe that they created the world (see pp.116–19). For many, the creator was an earthdiver, a turtle or other small creature who brought up mud from the depths of the primeval waters and fashioned the land from it (see pp.116–17). A Crow story tells how Old Man Coyote made the earth by blowing on a small lump of mud that ducks had brought from the bottom of the waters.

In Native belief, animals have spirits, just like human beings, and enjoy a complex reciprocal relationship with people, plants and the earth. Animals often play an important role in teaching people how to behave. Tricksters, for example, who frequently appear in the form of animals, provide their human neighbours with valuable moral lessons (see pp.120–23).

At the core of each Native culture is an abiding reverence for the region in which the people live. The landscape is sacred, a source of identity and strength. Alfonso Ortiz, a Tewa anthropologist, has spoken of how his grandmother instructed him to return home whenever he felt distant from his soul, in order to be spiritually refreshed by the four sacred mountains that mark the boundaries of the Tewa world.

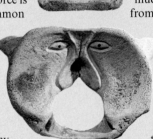

An image of a polar bear carved out of a washed-up whale vertebra by a 20th-century Inuit artist. The bear itself (top) has a spirit owner with human features, who is depicted on the reverse of the carving (below). The spirit owner's face is visually composed from the forms of two leaping killer whales.

BIG THUNDER SPEAKS OF THE EARTH

In early 1900, Bedagi, or Big Thunder, a famous orator of the Wabanakis (Micmac, Passamaquoddy, Penobscot and Maliseet), gave a speech on the relationship between nature, birth and death. There are numerous variations of the speech, but its central theme is clear: humans, animals and plants all come from the earth, are part of it and will ultimately return to it.

"The Great Spirit is our Father, but the earth is our Mother. She nourishes us. What we put in the ground she gives back to us, and healing plants as well. If we are wounded, we go to our Mother and seek to lay the wounded part against her, to be healed. When we hunt, no matter how powerful the bow, it is not our arrow that kills the moose; it is nature that kills him. The arrow sticks in his hide, and like all living things, he goes to our Mother to be healed by laying his wound against the earth, but this makes the arrow go further in.

"Meanwhile, I follow him. He is out of sight, but by putting my ear against a tree, I can hear when the moose makes his next leap, and I follow. Every time he stops and rubs his side the arrow is pushed in deeper. Eventually I find him, he is exhausted, and the arrow is driven clean through his body."

A Hopi kachina *(spirit) effigy made by William Quotskuyva in 1939. It represents the deity Masau'u, protector of the soil and also ruler of the dead, who were said to bring rain.*

The Badlands of South Dakota, a landscape of stark beauty that is sacred to the Sioux peoples. Followers of the Ghost Dance (see pp.136–7) fled here in 1890 before the massacre at Wounded Knee.

Kinship and spirit

For many Indian people, kinship was the key to the stability, integrity and survival of the community. For example, to be a nephew or a daughter was to possess a distinct role with well-defined rights and obligations to others. Those who came to villages as strangers – even white captives – were often adopted as "cousins" or "brothers", making their social position unambiguous and keeping the integrity of the group intact.

A particularly important role is played by elders. Traditionally, most child-rearing was done by grandparents, because it was considered that parents were too busy with daily life and did not yet possess enough wisdom to pass on to their children. Elders were, and are, the source of nurture and moral train-ing, and as storytellers, they are the repository of a people's mythological and spiritual inheritance. They, above all, are responsible for handing down the sacred traditions of a community.

Indian peoples often see their communities as an extension of the spirit-rich natural world. Clans (groups of families) and sacred societies (see pp.84–7) often believed that they were the descendants of an animal spirit, or totem, a word that anthropologists derived from the Ojibway *odem*, which may be translated as "village". The Iroquois peoples, for example, are divided into such groupings as Turtle Clan, Bear Clan and Wolf Clan, each headed by a Clan Mother. The totem animal may have assisted an ancestor in a hunt,

Clan chiefs were revered figures. This engraving of 1591 by Le Moyne illustrates Theodor de Bry's description of a funeral ceremony for a chief in the Northeast. Among other displays of grief, de Bry recounted, clan members fasted for three days and cut off most of their hair.

or helped him or her to find the way home. In other cases, a member of a clan may go on a quest to find an animal to adopt as the clan totem. For example, members of the Osage Spider Clan relate that a young man once went into the forest on just such an expedition. He was following some deer tracks when he fell over a large spider's web. The spider asked the man how he had come to trip over the web. He replied that he had been tracking a deer, because he was looking for a strong animal to be the symbol of his clan. The spider replied that, although he seemed to be a small, weak creature, he had the virtue of great patience. Furthermore, the spider said, all creatures came to him sooner or later, just as the man had done. Impressed by these words, the man returned to his clan, which adopted the spider as its totem.

Individuals who did not belong to a totem-based society or clan could develop their own relationship with a totem animal, which became their personal spirit guide. Clans and individuals were often thought to assume the characteristics of their spirit totem. For example, members of a Bear Clan might be said to possess great strength and ferocity. Mice are very shortsighted, and those who belonged to the Cheyenne Mouse Clan adopted a myopic view of the world: they paid careful attention to what happened nearby and at the present moment, but took little or no interest in anything distant or in the future.

A kiva (ceremonial chamber) built by the prehistoric Anasazi people at Mesa Verde Pueblo in Colorado. Present-day Pueblo peoples such as the Hopi believe that the totemic clan ancestors entrusted each clan with the care of a kiva and of the sacred rituals that are held in it.

Haida villages

The Queen Charlotte Islands, British Columbia, are the home of the Haida, who call the archipelago Haida Gwaii ("Islands of the People"). They are a proud, maritime people who derive great wealth from the sea, and their villages were once the most prosperous of the Northwest Coast. Until the arrival of Europeans in the 1770s, all 7,000 or so Haida lived in more than 30 shoreline villages of sturdy cedar-plank houses. Some settlements consisted of a small scattering of houses, while others extended along the shore for more than a mile (1.6km).

Haida houses, like others in the northern Northwest Coast region, were large and rectangular, and each was occupied by several related families. A typical house had corner posts, interior posts to support the roof beams, and walls, roof and floor of cedar planks. The planks were either lashed to the beams with rope or fastened with wooden dowels. There were sitting and sleeping platforms around the inside walls, with each family group separated by partitions of wood or cedar matting. Families were arranged by status, with the chief in the favoured location, at the end furthest from the door, and slaves by the doorway. Traditional Haida houses had a single, central hearth and no openings except a doorway and a smokehole in the roof. The doorway was sometimes cut through the body of a figure that was painted on the house front or carved in a totem pole. Such openings reflected the womb-like nature of the dwellings. Villages were mainly occupied in the winter. In the summer, people moved to temporary camps to harvest foods as they came into season.

HAIDA
VILLAGES

Pacific
Ocean

Colorado River

Mississippi

Rio Grande

North
Atlantic
Ocean

1 *The Haida village of Ninstints in the southern Queen Charlotte Islands, as it was in the 19th century. An outsider would have been struck by the forest of carved cedar poles among the houses of Haida villages. The Haida had more, and taller, poles than any other Northwest Coast peoples. There were three main types: the "totem pole", which showed the crest of the families within each house; the memorial pole, which was erected in memory of honoured ancestors (examples can be seen at far left and in the distance); and mortuary poles, on top of which rested chests that contained the remains of ancestors.*

2 **3** *The raising of a new totem pole in Yan, an abandoned village on Massett inlet, in 1991. European diseases, together with government and missionary resettlement programmes, led to the depopulation and abandonment of many Haida villages during the last decades of the 19th century. By 1900, the 1,000 or so surviving Haida had relocated to the missionary-run towns of Massett and Skidegate in the north of the Queen Charlotte Islands. Yan ceased to be inhabited after 1890. In 1991, descendants of Yan's last residents gathered at the old village for the ceremonial raising of this new totem pole representing the Bear Clan. The pole was carved from cedar by Jim Hart, one of a new generation of Native artists who, in the last 30 years or so, have dedicated themselves to the revival and preservation of the ancient carving skills of the Northwest Coast.*

4 *The deserted villages of the Haida soon fell into decay. Whites cut down the carved poles for firewood, shipped them out to museums or simply left them to rot where they stood, like these at Ninstints.*

Sacred societies

All but the smallest cultures tend to have ways of organizing themselves in groups other than those based primarily on kinship. For Native North Americans, such groupings most commonly took the form of sacred societies, associations based on a particular sacred ideal, ritual, being or object. They were sometimes directly linked with particular clans, but as often as not they crosscut kinship structures. Although the individual and his or her personal ritual life were important, membership of a sacred society provided a more distinct social identity. If these societies did not exist, or if they functioned improperly, the very survival of the people was feared to be in jeopardy.

Sacred societies drew their power from the spirit world. Often, as among the Kwakiutl, certain spirits took part in initiation rituals in the form of puppets or impersonators. Sometimes a society's power was centred on a sacred bundle of holy objects entrusted to its care by a tribe or clan. Sacred bundles were the focus of special ceremonies. For the Pawnee of the Plains, many sacred bundles were closely associated with the stars and contained symbols of

Kwakiutl puppets of wood, leather and hair representing the ghost No'tEmg.ila and its children. The puppets were used to embody these beings during the initiation rituals for the Warrior Spirit sacred society.

the cosmic forces. Alternatively, they might represent the psychological or elemental characteristics of the divinity to whom the bundle was consecrated. The bundle itself might be a piece of hide painted with star patterns that was wrapped around objects such as ears of corn (maize), representing the annual renewal of the earth. The Skull Bundle of the Skidi Pawnee originally contained what was said to be the skull of First Man. Later, after that skull broke, it held the skull of an important chief.

Societies of healers were especially prominent in the Northeast. The Huron dreaded sickness and therefore set great store by their curing societies. Each society had a leader whose office was hereditary; sometimes he was also an important chief. One curing society was the *atirenda*, which had about 80 members, including six women. In its principal dance, the *otakrendoiae*, the members pretended to kill one another with charms such as bears' claws, wolves' teeth or stones. The *atirenda* was especially skilled at curing ruptures.

Members of the Iroquois False Face Society wore "twisted face" masks to commemorate their guardian being, a giant who had once challenged the Creator to a test of strength by moving a mountain. The giant could barely shift it, but the Creator was so successful that the mountain hit the giant in the face before he was able to get out of the way. Chastened, the giant agreed to look after the health of the people from then on. However, his face remained in a permanent twisted grimace.

Sacred societies were an effective instrument of social control, providing a convenient way to educate youth and to allocate civic responsibilities and sacred obligations. Among some peoples, sacred societies played a central role in the running of the tribe. In North Carolina, the Eastern Cherokee (those who had escaped their people's forced relocation to Oklahoma; see p.45) closely coordinated their political activities with the cycle of major religious ceremonies. Tribal officials belonged to one of two sacred societies, the White Peace Organization or the Red War

This mask, worn by the False Face Society of Iroquois curers, depicts the legendary giant who was the source of their healing powers. His face was twisted in a collision with a mountain.

SACRED TEAM GAMES

Sometimes sacred societies specialized in playing a particular sport. Team games were certainly recreational activities, but like most aspects of Native life they also served a broader social and religious purpose.

The most widespread example of such a sport is the hoop and pole game. Played across the entire continent, the game was exclusively male and consisted basically of throwing a spear or shooting or throwing an arrow at a hoop or ring as it rolled along the ground. The hoop in particular possessed symbolic significance. The Zuni version of the game used a hoop strung with netting that symbolized the web of an ancestral protector being called Spider Woman.

The game was of great antiquity and there was remarkable diversity in both the implements used and the rules of play. The number of players varied, but there always seem to have been two teams, perhaps representing some fundamental duality, such as "we" (the people) and "they" (the unseen forces). When gambling was involved, as with the Arapaho, the takings were redistributed among team members.

The timing of matches was sometimes significant. For example, the Wasco of the Northwest Coast, played the game to mark the first salmon run of the season.

Organization. Chiefs of the White Peace Organization, together with their assistants and seven counsellors, formed a town's civil and religious tribunal. They were in charge of a ritual cycle which included several corn ceremonies, and the "Reconciliation", "New Moon" and "Bounding Bush" ceremonies. They also performed civic duties, acting as a criminal court, controlling marriage and divorce and training boys to hunt.

The Red War Organization ran all aspects of warfare, from the initial call-up of warriors to a body-count of the slain, and conducted purification rites before and after battle. The society was headed by a chief who was aided by various counsellors, surgeons, messengers and scouts, as well as by some older, highly respected matrons who were known as "Pretty Women". They had an important say in the conduct of warfare and in the fate of captives.

All-women societies existed alongside all-male ones. Among the Blackfeet of southern Alberta, women were acknowledged as the foundation of humanity, and ceremonies could not be run without them. Women kept the people's sacred bundles, without which the most important ceremonies, including the Sun Dance, could not take place. Only

SNAKE DANCERS

In the parched lands of the Southwest, rainmaking ceremonies are among the most significant events of the annual ritual calendar. The most important are conducted by specialist sacred societies, such as the Hopi Snake Dancers, whose week-long rites are held late in the summer every two years. The Hopi believe that the snake, with its zig-zag shape, is related to the lightning that heralds rain. The dances are intended as a great show of communal respect toward the snakes, so that they will bring enough rain for the growing harvest.

For the first four days of the ceremony, society members head north, south, east and west into the desert in order to catch snakes and bring them back to the village. There follow two days and nights on which primordial events are ritually re-enacted in a kiva, or ceremonial chamber, by members of the Hopi sacred societies. The remainder of the festival is taken up with races, dances (in which priests hold snakes in their mouths, even deadly rattlesnakes) and a final blessing. The snakes, which remain unharmed throughout the ceremony, are then gathered up and released back into the wild.

Hopi Snake Dancers blessing the snakes, 1911. Photographs of the Snake Dances became so popular among white Americans at the end of the 19th century that the army of competing photographers often outnumbered the dancers and disrupted the sacred rituals. In the end, the Hopi imposed a ban – in force to this day – on all photography by outsiders during the ceremonies.

women were permitted to open the bundles and hand the sacred objects over to men, and only women could call up the spirits. Prior to the Sun Dance, members of the Old Women's Society built a ceremonial lodge in the shape of a buffalo corral. On the fourth day of the ceremony, they re-enacted a buffalo drive into the corral, with some members wearing bison headdresses and mimicking the animal. The event was staged in honour of the Creator spirit, the buffalo and the history of the people.

Sometimes sacred societies controlled very specific ceremonies. For the Crow of the northwestern Plains, the Tobacco Society was responsible for the Tobacco Ceremony, which was thought crucial to the prosperity of the tribe. It was also thought that the Crow would survive only if they continued to plant seeds from the originally cultivated plants. The ceremony began with the ritual planting of seeds by a Tobacco Planter. This role was hereditary, but a person could purchase the right to become a Planter. The planting ritual included abstention from food and water for several days, as well as cutting or burning the arms and chest. In exchange for the honour of planting the seeds, a Planter had to give up all worldly possessions.

Ceremonial transformations

For Native North Americans, the boundaries between the world of the spirits and the world of living people were not clearly defined: a third, "in-between" world of transition separated them. Every entity to some degree inhabited all three worlds. If a human possessed the power or carried out appropriate rituals, he or she could be transformed into a being from one of the other two worlds.

This Haida mask portrays the evil Cannibal Spirit. At a certain point in a dance, the mask opens to release a human whom the spirit has possessed.

Such transformations often duplicated events of the "beginning time", when the world came to be as it is through the agency of culture heroes and tricksters (see pp.120–23). On cere-monial occasions, an individual might assume the appearance of such a figure and be thought literally to become that being. When a Blackfoot holy man put on a yellow bear hide, for his audience he actually *was* the bear.

For the Kwakiutl and Haida of the Northwest Coast, the supernatural beings that shaped the world in the beginning time often changed themselves into animal or human form or took possession of people. Such beings were not always benign. In some dances, elaborately painted two-layered masks were used to illustrate the shapeshifting. The outside

In this painting by modern Apache artist Pablita Velarde, male Chiricahua Apache dancers assume the guise of the Ga'an, benevolent mountain spirits who bestow blessings during important ceremonies.

mask might depict the head of a salmon. During the dance, the dancer pulled a string to open the mask and reveal an inner mask depicting the *sisi-utl*, a fearsome dragon-like creature. Conversely, the mask of a malign spirit might open at some point to reveal the face of the human who until that point had been possessed by the being.

Transformation commonly occurs in "animal-calling" ceremonies, such as the Deer-Calling ceremonies of the Pueblo peoples, in which men dress as deer. At dawn, hunters call to the deer from the hills, and the shadowy forms of deer-men on all fours emerge into the new sunlight with shaking antlers and hides. They leap about and play before the people while little boys, dressed as fawns, prance around them. The deer-dancers are escorted by a figure known as Mother of Game, who leads the "deer" to the hunters, where they are symbolically killed.

SACRED CLOWNS

Many groups possess respected specialists referred to as "sacred clowns", who at sacred ceremonies would undergo transformation into disruptive, clownish figures. For example, during the Mandan Okipa ceremony (see p.81), a figure called Foolish One would bring great delight to the audience by imitating a mating male buffalo bull before being unceremoniously driven from the village.

The clowns' behaviour was often intended to be instructive, teaching by bad example. The Zuni *Koyemshi* warned against greed by their grotesque gluttony. The Lakota *Heyoka* were more obviously comic. For example, they might ride a horse while facing backwards or swim in icy water and complain how hot it was.

A young Hopi koshare, *or sacred clown, photographed in 1973 during "Indian Day" at his school in Arizona.*

The powwow

The term "powwow" probably derives from the Algonquian word *pauau*, meaning a gathering of people. European Americans use the term to describe any meeting or social event at which issues of importance are discussed. For Indians, however, the powwow refers to a traditional large tribal or intertribal secular gathering that encompasses singing, dancing, giveaways and honouring ceremonies. Powwows are dramatic and public expressions of Indian identity. Sometimes they are open to the general public, but more often they are geared toward Indians themselves. Intertribal powwows are obviously larger than tribal ones, but whatever their size, the powwow is an important vehicle for handing down Indian traditions from one generation to the next.

At a powwow held in Browning, Montana, dancers participate in a colourful ceremonial display that includes traditional songs and dances in imitation of animals and natural forces.

There is a well-established "powwow highway", or circuit, and Indians travel across the country from late spring to early autumn in order to take part in intertribal powwows. As pan-Indian events, these powwows enable tribal members to foster close relations with other tribes, and they are therefore a demonstration of Native North American solidarity as well as a powerful expression of Indian culture.

The event, which is focused on a central arena, or "arbour", usually begins with a grand entrance. The opening procession is often led by military veterans, who conduct a flag-raising ceremony and brief invocation. War dances usually follow, along with other types of dances, such as round dances, grass dances and rabbit dances. Many of these dances are specifically designated as intertribal. Colourfully costumed, with shawls, beadwork, bustles or elaborate headgear, powwow dancers proceed gracefully around the arena, a steady drumbeat directing their movements. Many powwows include dance competitions (see below). Contestants often travel great distances to attend these events, which offer substantial cash prizes for dancers and drummers.

Another powwow highlight is the giveaway ceremony, at which one individual or family presents another with gifts that may be as elaborate as the handmade "star" quilts of the Sioux or as simple as kitchen utensils. A giveaway ceremony is one way of acknowledging people in the community who have distinguished themselves, such as university graduates, military personnel and community leaders. Someone who has helped a family during a crisis, such as a period of mourning, might also be honoured. Giveaways usually take place in the afternoon, between dances. The powwow announcer will state the reason for the giveaway, who the donors and recipients are, and will then call for an honour dance. The participants then shake hands and the programme of powwow dancing resumes.

At a powwow, socializing is as important as dancing. It is an occasion for Indians who may belong to many different tribes to renew old friendships, and they may sit down together for a feast at which traditional Native North American foods, such as bison, venison, corn (maize) stew and fry bread, are served. There may be prayers and political speeches, and people sometimes take advantage of the occasion to make extra money by selling handicrafts.

DANCE COMPETITIONS

Dance competitions have categories depending on style of dance, age and sex, and may include "traditional", "fancy", "grass", "shawl" and "jingle dress" dancing. Entrants wear different styles of clothing according to the dance. For example, a male fancy dancer dons feather bustles and beads, while a female shawl dancer wears a long-fringed shawl over an elaborately beaded dress, moccasins and leggings. Jingle dress dancers are so-called from the tin bells that adorn their costumes. The judges, who are usually former powwow dance champions, mingle among the competitors and judge mastery of style as well as ability to keep time with the song and to end on the last drumbeat. The winners often dance a short solo in front of a cheering crowd.

Holy people

Individual religious practices that are based on a personal spirit or totem play an important part in the daily lives of most Native North Americans. However, certain people appear to have greater contact with the spirit world than others. The word "shaman" is widely used by anthropologists to refer to such individuals. A shaman is a religious specialist who has acquired exceptional powers to deal with the supernatural, usually after he or she has been seized by spirits. However, many Native North Americans dislike "shaman" as a blanket term because it derives from a foreign culture – the Tungus people, reindeer herders of eastern Siberia – and does not encompass the diversity of Native specialists. These are probably best referred to as "holy people".

A shell plaque depicting a shamanistic figure with a severed head in one hand and a ritual wand in the other. Found in Tennessee, the plaque dates from the Mississippian culture (c. AD 1000) and may have been part of a holy person's paraphernalia.

Holy people range from a person who, without especially seeking it, has just one powerful vision that provides guidance for the future, to a nearly full-time practitioner who is in constant communication with the spirits and capable of manipulating the surrounding world. The first category includes the famous war chiefs Sitting Bull and Crazy Horse, who were often thought of as holy men by their people. They used their limited contacts with the spirit world for the benefit of their people, especially in warfare. They certainly would not be considered as shamans, which might be an appropriate term for the second type of holy person: one who attempts to influence or even impose his or her will on the supernatural, like the Yaqui shaman who seeks to transform his body into that of an animal.

Outsiders often call holy people "medicine men" or "medicine women", but these terms are sometimes used pejoratively. However, they might be appropriate when a holy person's power of vision is associated with the diagnosis and curing of illness.

Holy people are seen as a special point of contact between the natural world and the world of spirits. In general, they would act for the good of their people. Sometimes they may use their abilities to harm individuals or groups identified as the people's enemies.

Among the most important tasks of holy people is to provide for the physical well-being of their people by preventing, diagnosing and curing illness. The causes for illness were many. For example, sickness might be the result of sorcery or witchcraft. The Western Apache believed that some of the most serious illnesses were caused by improper behaviour toward holy things. Maladies struck when someone violated the taboos surrounding things in which sacred power was believed to dwell. For example, boiling a deer's stomach, eating its tongue or cutting its tail off a hide offended Deer Power. Stepping on a snake's tail or leaning against a tree

BECOMING A HOLY PERSON

Among the Crow, most adult men actively sought visionary power. They would engage in bodily deprivation, even self-torture, in their attempt to receive visions. If they succeeded, they would expect to gain special power in battle or to acquire wealth. Most seekers would never have a vision, so there was no social stigma attached to failure.

For the Washo of the Great Basin, holy power came unsought and unwanted. The first signs appeared in a series of dreams in which an animal or a ghost might feature. This vision would offer power for life. The Washo feared such power because it was dangerous, and the better defined the power, the more dangerous it became. A man might ignore the offer, but in this case a spirit being, or *wegaleyo*, might inflict ailments on the dreamer. When the subject finally relented, the *wegaleyo* would instruct him in dreams. In particular, it would tell him his own unique holy song or chant, the objects to be used in ceremonies, and the location of a secret pool for ritual ablution and other sacred practices. The subject would be required to seek out a recognized holy man who could instruct him in the arts of sleight of hand, ventriloquy and other skills needed for ceremonies.

Among the Upper Skagit people of Washington State, shamans became known only when they started practising publicly. They themselves chose whether or not to become shamans, after acquiring the necessary spirits through fasting or visions. Many Upper Skagit holy people waited to acquire spirit power until they reached middle age, when they might inherit the shamanistic spirit of a deceased parent or brother.

This photograph of 1908 shows a group of Arikara "Mother Night Men" returning home to their village, probably after a nightlong ceremony at a sacred earth lodge. Members of the "Medicine Fraternity" of holy men, the Mother Night Men are carrying rattles used in their sacred rituals.

that had been hit by lightning would also cause sickness. Taboos against urinating in water or defecating in a cornfield had an obvious practical value.

When someone fell ill, a holy person was called in to find the cause and to cure the sickness. Among the Western Apache, curing ceremonials were community endeavours. The holy person or another elder would tell stories surrounding the origin of the ritual in order to focus the minds of the audience and to reaffirm their belief in the powers that were at work. The ceremony itself began dramatically, with fires and beating drums. Following this, the holy person would enter the patient's dwelling, sit by the fire and chant, while the patient sat motionless for nearly two hours. There was then a break, in which the curer and the audience ate and drank *tulpai*, a fermented corn beverage, while the patient struggled to remain awake. In the small hours of the morning, at about 3am, the chanting started again, invoking the powers of the Black-tailed Deer and the beings known as the *Ga'an*. As dawn broke, the holy person stopped chanting, sprinkled the patient's head and shoulders with cattail pollen and then stroked his or her forehead with lightning grass. Exhausted, the holy person then sang two more chants, and the ceremony came to an end.

Among the Athapaskan Tanaina of the Subarctic, a holy man would accumulate a variety of spiritual helpers for curing. He might dream of natural objects with medicinal properties, which he would then collect and carry in a pouch. A Tanaina holy man had a range of ritual "tools" at his disposal, such as spiritual songs, drums, rattles and masks. Curing involved a ceremonial performance to frighten away the evil spirits that caused sickness. Crucial to the process was an ability to go into a trance and converse with the spirit world. With the help of a particular guardian spirit, the holy man was able to ascertain which spirit had caused the problem; he would then intimidate it with a show of his power. Curing often involved the removal of a solid object pulled or sucked from the patient, such as a stone, a piece of string or a bullet. The curer was paid for his treatment by the patient's family.

Many holy people use medicinal plants in their practice. Sleight of hand is involved in many plant cures, but a

YUWIPI

Performed for specific diagnostic purposes, the Lakota *yuwipi* curing ceremony requires strict adherence to ritual form. For example, participants take care to avoid contamination, especially contact with menstruating women. They must be open and receptive:

any scepticism can cause the ceremony to fail.

To begin with, blankets and quilts cover the windows to exclude all light. Helpers bind the holy person and roll him up in canvas or a blanket. In total darkness, spirits are seen as flashes of light, eagles appear to fly across the room and participants hear wings flapping or feel them

brushing their cheeks. These spirits are credited with the success of the ceremony. If a *yuwipi* is successful, the holy person will experience a vision that will reveal the cause or source of a patient's illness and suggest a course of treament. Holy people who have particularly clear and powerful *yuwipi* visions are highly respected.

Tek-'ic, a Yakutat Tlingit shaman, c.1888. BELOW *Some ritual tools used by Tlingit shamans. The objects were believed to possess great power, as was the shaman's long hair.*

Eagle-spirit mask (19th century).

Club with human and animal figures (19th century).

Ceremonial rattle (pre-1800).

Bone spirit charm (19th century).

holy person is not simply a conjurer: he possesses a substantial knowledge, gained through apprenticeship, of herbs and plants that are pharmacologically active and can effect medical cures.

Another type of holy person is the diviner. Divination is an esoteric religious activity, practised by a few who are especially gifted. Simply put, it is a way of finding things out: a diviner can discover the cause of witchcraft or sorcery, help to find something that has been lost or stolen, and predict the outcome of a hunting party.

The diviner might help a healer to discover which taboo his patient has broken, and he might also prescribe the correct procedure for a patient's treatment, down to the timing of rituals and which holy person to call upon for assistance. In the Northeast, the Huron had three types of diviner who were highly respected and well paid for their work. One type found lost objects, another could predict future events and the third cured sickness. Those who dealt with the sick were called *ocata* or *saokata*. Each had his *oki*, or familiar spirit, which often revealed the illness to the diviner in a dream. On other occasions, the diviner might seek revelations by gazing into a bowl of water or into a fire. Some diviners went into a frenzy, fasted or secluded themselves in a dark sweat-house.

The most common form of divination among the Navajo is "hand-trembling". When a person falls ill, an intermediary (usually a member of the patient's family) makes the contact with a holy per-

SHAKING TENT

The Ojibway know that human help is not always sufficient and that people sometimes need to call upon sacred beings to give answers to problems. They have many ways of interacting with these beings, or "grandfathers", which are regarded as a very real presence in Ojibway life. The divination lodge known as "Shaking Tent" is one method of coming into direct contact with them. The "tent" itself is a barrel-like framework of poles about seven feet (2m) high. It is set up outdoors and covered with canvas, skins or birch bark. In it, divination or conjuring is used to discover the cause of illness or to find a lost object. After dark, the

conjurer enters the tent and calls on the beings that are his own *pawaganak*, or guardian spirits. The souls of

living beings (other than humans) and the dead may be invoked, and their arrival is signalled when the tent is shaken by the spirits embodying the Winds. No human action is involved – sometimes the conjurer may even be tied up with rope.

Spirit voices are then heard to come from the tent, often naming themselves or singing a song; they might be animals or well-known characters from myths. At this point, those in attendance can sometimes talk directly to the beings to seek answers to their questions.

A fanciful 19th-century drawing of a Shaking Tent, showing the arrival of various spirit beings.

A present-day Navajo holy person cleanses his hands with yucca root, a natural soap commonly used for ritual washing before curing ceremonies, weddings and other sacred occasions.

son known as a hand-trembler, arranges the time of the visit and offers a fee. The hand-trembler sits down by the patient. After washing his hands and arms, he takes pollen, and working from right to left, puts it on the soles of the patient's feet, then on the knees, palms, breast, between the shoulders, on top of the head and in the mouth.

Next, the curer sits about three feet (1m) to the right of the patient. He takes more pollen and, starting at a vein on the inside of his own right elbow, traces it along his arm, down to the tips of his fingers. As he does this, he prays: "Black Gila Monster, please tell me what is wrong with this patient. I am giving you a jet bead to tell me what illness he has." He repeats the prayer for every finger, each time assigning a new colour to both the gila monster (a type of lizard) and to the bead. He then sings a "gila monster song", during which his hand and arm tremble, sometimes violently. He interprets the trembling to discover the information that he seeks.

When hand-trembling is used for purposes other than diagnosing illness, the client is not present. For lost items, a piece of clothing is used. For a theft, a hand-trembler can be led to the suspect and will grasp him by the shoulder.

Seeking the spirit

According to many Native North American traditions, some people will never be able to traverse the indistinct line dividing the world of the spirits from the world in which people live. However, those who possess special gifts or a characteristic that is appreciated by the spirit world will find the boundary no barrier. Some groups fear the spirit world and endeavour to avoid it. Others, in contrast, actively seek to make contact with it and the powers that it confers. For yet others, the power of the spirits comes unbidden.

Spirit power is a mysterious force that derives from everything in nature. The few Indian groups that offer a description of it say that it is immaterial and gives off a bright, white light like the sun. They believe that people who do not possess spirit power are ineffectual and weak, but that when they acquire it they become strong and capable.

The spirits and spirit power are commonly said to come in visions. These might be sought on solitary vision quests, especially among Plains peoples (see box, opposite). Individuals participating in certain ceremonies, such as the

Sun Dance (see pp.112–13), could also receive a vision through ritual purification, self-deprivation through fasting, or physical pain. In millennarian movements such as the Ghost Dance (see pp.136–7), a vision of another, better world came to some through physical exhaustion from dancing. The ingestion of the peyote cactus accompanied by communal singing and drumming (see p.130) can also induce a vision.

Power sometimes comes from the possession of a certain object. For example, many Plains and Southwestern groups believed that the circular, leather-covered frame of a shield, made with the help of a holy person, symbolized the world and could attract the protection of the spirits. To enhance its power, the shield might be adorned with feathers or other sacred objects, or with painted symbols representing images in a dream or vision. The precise process of manufacture also affected the shield's power for protection.

Unsought spirits came most frequently in dreams. Among groups such as the Mohave of the Southwest or the Iroquois of the Northeast, it is believed

A Sioux, Leonard Crow Dog, emerges from a sweat lodge (a steam hut). A crucial stage in seeking a vision was the ritual purification undergone in a sweat lodge. The vision seeker would sit in the lodge and create steam by dousing hot rocks with water. After bathing, he or she would scrape off perspiration using twigs or branches. Sweat lodges are still widely used for relaxation and healing as well as for spiritual purposes.

that dreams are able to channel power directly from the spirit world to the individual. For the Menominee of the Great Lakes region, all dreams had significance, and the prophecies or warnings that they might contain were always scrupulously observed. For example, if a man frequently dreamed of drowning, he would take care to make a small canoe as a talisman and carry it about with him at all times. If the meaning of a dream was unclear, a person sought the interpretation of an elder, who, being nearer the end of life, was believed to be closer to the world of spirits. Anyone who had a dream that could not be interpreted, or who did not dream at all, was considered to be cut off from the power of the spirits (see also pp.130–31).

VISION QUESTS

For many tribes, the most common way of seeking to contact the spirits and receive their power is through a lone vision quest. A person may seek a spiritual vision several times during his or her life, even at an advanced age, although it is traditionally a more common activity among the young. The Upper Skagit of western Washington State believe that spirits can be contacted at any age, but traditionally parents send their children out on vision quests from about the age of four until puberty. Most Indian nations believe that it is important for both girls and boys to experience a vision and acquire spirit power.

To receive spirits, an individual first has to be clean both internally and externally, which is achieved by solitary fasting and bathing in a sweat lodge (see picture opposite). The length of the fast is directly related to the power of the spirit that was sought.

Children receive guidance about which spirit they are to seek. For example, a boy might be told to take a bow on a quest to help him receive a vision of a hunting spirit. If the quest is successful, the child is not supposed to acknowledge it publicly until he or she is older. It is also important that young people call upon the aid of the newly-acquired power only in serious situations.

Medicine Deer Rock in Montana, where the Sioux chief Sitting Bull (see p.32) came on a vision quest and experienced a premonition of his victory at the Little Bighorn in 1876.

Rites of passage

Most Native North American cultures mark the important times of transition in a person's life – birth, puberty and adolescence, marriage and death – with important rituals during which the passage from the old state to the new is formally enacted. At such times of physical transition, the person is believed to be particulary close to the spirit world. It is a state that is fraught with both danger and great potential.

Unborn and newborn children are especially vulnerable, and many tribes traditionally observed taboos to keep infants from harm. For example, a pregnant Cherokee woman would not eat speckled trout for fear that her child would have facial blemishes. Apache women avoided eggs, which they believed might cause a child to be born blind, and animal tongue, which might make a child slow to talk.

The most dramatic rites of passage in many cultures accompany the move from childhood to adulthood. Such rites are broadly similar in structure in most Native cultures and, indeed, in tribal societies throughout the world. They often include a period of physical isolation, marking the point at which a person severs the links with his or her former status. This brief exile from society represents an interim state of "not-being", and often involves a test of physical endurance, pain or deprivation. The whole process usually ends with a ritual completing one's incorporation into the new status group. The *Nozihzho* ("Stand Sleeping") rite of the Omaha included most of these

elements. It was a four-day fasting rite undergone by all Omaha adolescent males (and by any female who so desired). The name refers to the trance experienced by the youths in the course of the rite. In it, they became oblivious to the outside world and conscious only of their inner being. The rite re-created the Omaha origin myth. The boy would find an isolated spot, where he would spread clay over his head in honour of the animals who went to the bottom of a great body of water and brought up mud from which the earth was created (see p.117). He prayed to Wakoda, the mysterious power that controlled all of nature. The boy filled his mind with thoughts of health, successful hunting and war, and a happy, long life, but it was taboo to ask for special favours.

Wakoda, it was believed, would respond with a vision or dream that would include a sacred song. Dreams of hawks, elks or thunder might bring great fortune. The song was a good luck charm connecting the boy to the powers of the universe. He could use it throughout his lifetime as a way to call for help from guardian spirits in time of crisis.

On his return from the rite, the boy would rest for four days before seeking the advice of an elder who had had a similar dream. Next, the boy would find and kill the creature that had appeared in his dream-vision, keeping a part of it as a sacred possession for his personal

A Plains Indian beaded buckskin pouch in the form of a turtle. It was made to contain a baby's umbilical cord and was fixed to the cradle. Later in life, the pouch was worn as a talisman.

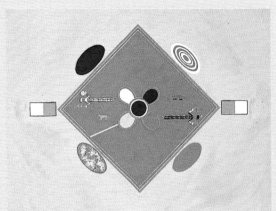

WARRIOR "COUPS"

In the course of his career as a warrior, a Dakota Sioux male enhanced his military status by accomplishing various "coups" – acts that demonstrated his bravery in battle. Each category of coup entitled the warrior to wear a different style of feather, trimmed, clipped or dyed according to the coup. Some of these are shown below.

Feather dyed red: Wounded in battle.

Feather with red spot: Killed an enemy.

Feather with notch: Cut an enemy's throat and scalped him.

Feather clipped: Cut an enemy's throat.

Feather with jagged edge: Accomplished four coups.

Feather partly stripped: Accomplished five coups.

WOMEN'S POWER

As the bringer of life, a woman was a microcosm of Mother Earth. For this reason, women were venerated and their power was sometimes feared. Like other periods of transition when the body was in a state of physical and spiritual instability, a girl's first menstruation was considered to be a time of extraordinary power and potential danger.

Rites of passage marking the first period usually included the girl's isolation in a small menstrual hut set apart from the village. She was also instructed on the many taboos she would have to observe during subsequent menstruations. One reason for such taboos was the belief that menstrual blood was an especially dangerous substance, and that if it came into contact with sacred objects it could rob them of power and bring illness. For many women this was a strict

A sandpainting used in Kinaalda, *the Navajo puberty rite for girls. It represents the first* Kinaalda, *held to mark the menstruation, just four days after her birth, of a figure called Changing Woman, the daughter of First Man and First Woman and ancestor of the Navajo.* Kinaalda, *which is practised to this day, forms part of Blessingway, a cycle of ceremonies that encompasses all the Navajo rites of passage.*

regimen, because it meant that there were several days each month when they would be unable to fulfil their daily tasks. However, it was also a time of rest and regeneration.

The Lakota referred to the the spell of seclusion during menstruation as *isanti*, or "dwelling alone". They believed that menstruation was a form of natural purification, which meant that a woman did not need to go to the sweat lodge (see p.98) for regular ritual purification as a man did.

medicine bundle. He would carry the object to war or use it during rituals.

The *Nozihzho* ritual was not without its dangers. A dream of snakes could spell trouble. If the boy dreamed of the moon and awoke at the wrong time, he would have to abandon the idea of becoming a man and take up the ways of a woman, living as a *mixuga* who was instructed by the moon. As a *mixuga*, he would dress like a woman and wear his hair long, instead of in a man's roach (with the head shaved except for a strip from nape to brow). He would not hunt and fight, but till, plant and harvest like a woman, and practise a woman's crafts.

Courtship involved its own special customs. For example, Lakota men serenaded young women with specially made courting flutes, which were often carved with animals – usually birds known for their showy courtship "dances", such as ducks, cranes and prairie chickens. Often made by holy people, the flutes were thought to possess powerful magic notes that would cause the woman to travel anywhere with her lover.

Native North Americans often viewed marriage as a state that would endure until death, and the marriage rites of some peoples clearly reflect this. Traditional Hopi weddings started at dawn. The couple would sprinkle corn (maize) meal over the eastern boundary of their mesa, toward the rising sun. The groom's family would then weave for the bride two white cotton wedding robes with fringed sashes. The bride would wear only one robe during the wedding: the other was her burial shroud. The twin garments therefore confirmed a woman's marital status and also eased her way into the spirit world at death.

A Lakota warrior courts a young woman in this late 19th-century Indian drawing in a ledger. Both wear their finest attire and sport parasols in accordance with contemporary Plains Indian fashion.

DEATH AND THE AFTERLIFE

Indian customs and beliefs about the end of life varied from nation to nation, but many peoples thought that an individual had at least two souls. One was free and could leave the body during dreams or illness, while the other was corporeal and remained with the body at all times. The first soul went to the afterlife after death; the second died with the body, or was at least bound to it for an indeterminate time after death.

For the Navajo, death happened when the wind of life that came into a body at birth departed. Deaths were generally feared, because while a dead person's goodness contributed to the balance and harmony of the universe, bad qualities remained behind in the form of a ghost who could bring harm to the living.

The people most threatened by the dead were those closest to them in life, and so, among the Tlingit of the Northwest Coast, mortuary rituals were often handled by those of a different kinship group. As happened to people during other rites of passage, the dead were placed apart and their connections with the living world severed. Among the Yuma of the Southwest,

This bowl, made by prehistoric Indians of the Mimbres River valley, New Mexico, was "killed" by piercing before being placed in a grave. According to one theory, this released the figure depicted on the bowl, who then accompanied the dead person into the afterworld.

this was accomplished by burning the residence of the dead, or, if relatives continued to live there, by creating a new door or smokehole so that the dead could not find their way back into the house. A corpse was disposed of by cremation, burial in an earth mound, or placement on a scaffold under the open sky. The Lakota *wanagi* ("things of the shadow") spirits are said to

guard graves and can cause harm if the dead are disturbed.

Most nations believed in an afterlife, but it was not always the stereotypical "happy hunting grounds" to which Indians were commonly said to go after death. In most cases, it was believed that one of the dead person's souls would eventually join the Creator for eternity. Among the Delaware, it was believed that the corporeal soul passed through 12 cosmic layers before doing so.

Often, the afterworld was a stopover before a soul was reincarnated. For other peoples, the afterlife was a reversal of the world of the living, where rivers ran backwards, seasons were mixed up and people danced with crossed feet.

Because the dead often suffered anguish at being separated from the living, the living endeavoured to ease their pain. To demonstrate how much a person was missed, some might mourn by slashing themselves or cutting off a fingertip. Many grieved for a period and others carried out simple, gentle ceremonies, such as offering food to ease the dead person's passage into the afterlife. Sometimes people were prepared for death from an early age, as in the case of Hopi brides (see opposite).

Celebrating the past

Almost every Native North American ritual represents a celebration of the past, but not always in a way that glorifies specific events as spectacular or unique. Typically Western events, such as the celebration of a country's independence day, primarily commemorate individual events in a past that may be recent or remote, but always removed from the present. But Native ceremonies and rituals acknowledge more than just the particular context in which they are held, or the re-enacted sacred events that they may incorporate. In accordance with Native concepts of the "living past" (see pp.12–13), they celebrate the whole of the past as an active, invisible presence in the life of the people.

Ritual acknowledgments of the past may be very simple, individual and personal. For example, every morning, a Western Shoshoni holy woman rises just before dawn and prays to the east. Each phrase of her prayer ends with, "Now, then, bless the people." The simple phrase "now, then" represents a thanksgiving for the continuation of her own life, a recognition of the cycles of nature, and a commemoration of her people's past and journey into the future.

Some commemorations may take the form of traditional communal festivals, such as the potlatch (see p.62). The Kwakiutl potlatch includes songs, dances and sacred rites that have altered little over the centuries. For hundreds of

THE SACRED PIPE

Indian peoples have used pipes in ceremonies for generations. The sacred pipe is one means by which the people's connection with the past remains vital. It represents the centre of the cosmos. To celebrate the pipe

is to return to a time when the spirits entered the world of humans and gave a profound gift. The smoke from a pipe may carry prayers to the ancestors.

The Lakota say that their sacred pipe came to them from a beautiful spirit-being called White Buffalo Calf

Woman. Two Lakota hunters saw her and one desired her. But a cloud covered him and, when it lifted, only a pile of bones remained. She came to the tribe and gave them a sacred red pipe, saying: "Behold this pipe! Remember always how sacred it is and treat it as such, for it will take you to the end. Remember, in me there are four ages. I am leaving, but will look back on your people in every age, and in the end I will return." Since then, the Buffalo Calf Pipe has been held by the Keeper of the Sacred Pipe, a member of the Looking Horse family, who now live on the Cheyenne River Reservation in South Dakota.

An Ojibway dancer prays with a pipe at the Grand Portage powwow, Minnesota.

During winter ceremonies, Kwakiutl dancers wore masks that commemorated the totemic animal ancestors of clans and families. Those portrayed by the masked dancers in this early 20th-century picture by Edward Curtis, one of the most renowned photographers of Native North American subjects, are the raven, sea eagle, "wild man", mountain goat, grizzly bear, bee, wasp and killer whale.

years, it has also marked the transfer of power from one generation to the next. Valued material objects, such as a large, flat piece of copper incised with the image of a totemic animal, are handed over to a new chief as a symbol of his power and of its transmission from the ancestors and other beings in the past.

Other celebrations combine ancient elements with new formats. An example is the annual Choctaw Fair, held every summer on the Pearl River Reservation in Mississippi by the descendants of Choctaws who refused to move from their ancestral homelands in the 19th century. Choctaws come from all over the US to commemorate their past, traditions and very survival as a nation.

The fair, held at around the time that the Choctaw used to hold a ceremony for the ripening of the corn (maize), includes storytelling, dancing and the traditional ball game *ishtaboli*.

Also of relatively recent origin but containing ancient elements are the annual Eskimo-Indian Olympics at Fairbanks, Alaska, founded in 1961. A four-day programme of traditional activities includes the Knuckle Hop, in which participants bounce on their knuckles over the floor in imitation of a seal on an ice floe. Many spectators and competitors are urban Indians and Inuit for whom the games and their accompanying activities provide an essential connection with their traditional past.

The Great Serpent Mound

Above Brush Creek in Adams County, Ohio, a large serpentine earthwork loops and coils along the top of a prominent ridge, surrounded by steep wooded slopes and a sheer cliff. Known as the Great Serpent Mound, it is a low, rounded bank, more than 1,250 feet (381m) long, 20 feet (6m) wide and 4 feet (1.2m) high. The mound resembles a snake uncoiling as it moves across the ground, with seven extended coils and three still curled in the tail.

It is not known who constructed this monumental earthwork, but it is probably the work of the Adena culture, which flourished in the region between *c*.500BC and *c*.AD200. Although no datable artefacts have been found at the serpent itself, a conical burial mound that has been definitely associated with the Adena stands only 400 feet (122m) away. Mound-building was a significant feature of both the Adena and the later Hopewell cultures.

By 1886, the mound had become badly scarred by treasure-hunters and sightseers, and soil erosion had also taken its toll. The monument seemed likely to be turned into a cornfield until P.W. Putnam of the Peabody Museum at Harvard University rescued the site and restored it.

The Great Serpent Mound became part of a state park in 1900, and a viewing platform was erected for visitors to the site. However, despite this official status, the monument is presently under threat from land developers, who want to dam Brush Creek and build an artificial lake and resort community near the site, and from oil and mining companies, who would destroy the mound in the search for gas, oil and uranium.

Pacific
Ocean

Colorado River

Rio Grande

Mississippi

● SERPENT MOUND

North
Atlantic
Ocean

1 *An aerial view of the Great Serpent Mound today. The earthwork is so long that it can be seen in its entirety only from the sky. The scale of the construction indicates that the makers were highly organized and efficient, because an enormous communal effort would have been required to heap thousands of tons of earth – probably by the basketful – to create the effigy. It may have taken hundreds of people many years to finish it.*

2 *This engraving of the Serpent Mound appeared in 1848 in* Ancient Monuments of the Mississippi Valley *by E. G. Squier and E. H. Davis, the first archaeologists to survey the earthwork. Their report, commissioned by the Smithsonian Institution in Washington, D.C., provoked a flood of visitors, who inflicted serious damage before Putnam restored the monument.*

3 *The serpent effigy appears to hold a large, oval object in its jaws, and it has been suggested that the earthwork may represent a snake eating an egg, like the Texas rat snake shown here. Snakes play an important role in many Native North American cultures, and this has prompted a number of theories regarding the significance of the earthwork. However, in the absence of substantial evidence, ideas about the precise purpose and function of the Great Serpent Mound must remain no more than speculation.*

4 *It appears likely that the earthwork was the work of the Adena culture, which is named from another site in Ohio. The Adena and the Hopewell culture, which emerged in the Illinois-Ohio region a few centuries later, built large burial mounds for high-status individuals. Grave goods such as this Adena bird claw of mica illustrate the sophistication of both cultures.*

Honouring the animals

For Native North Americans, the relationship between people and animals is profound and complex. Many peoples believed themselves to be the direct descendants of animals, or at least, that animals were relatives of the people. Animals are therefore entitled to the rights and respect due to human kin. Above all, people must honour the animals because they are willing to give their lives in order that humans can live.

According to the Koyukon of Alaska, animals understand that people must hunt them to live and they are not offended by this. But they insist at all times that they be treated humanely, whether they are being hunted or not. A

starving moose, stuck in deep snow, should be fed every day until it gains enough strength to pull itself free and walk away. The Koyukon understand that an animal and its spirit are the same thing. The spirit is both individual to the animal but also part of the collective spirit of the species. This means that when one animal is offended, all members of its species may become aloof from the hunter.

The proper treatment of the animal spirits also involves hundreds of rules and taboos that affect a hunter's good fortune. Luck is regarded as a powerful force that binds humanity to the animal spirits. The Koyukon must honour the animals by observing the rules, or their luck may desert them. If this happens, the people may not survive. For example, boasting about what has not yet happened may cause the opposite to occur: thus, someone who says he will trap many beavers will suddenly find that he cannot catch any. A man who brags about his bear-hunting prowess may end up being mauled by a bear.

The White Beaver Ritual of the Chawi band of the Pawnee honoured animals at a potent time, when they awoke from hibernation. After the winter, it was believed, the animals had new life put into them by the gods. If the proper ritual was observed, some of the divine power could pass to the doctors, who could use it for the benefit of the people. The ritual was run largely by doctors, who formed the third-ranking

A Yaqui deer-dancer of southern Arizona. The Yaqui, who live in Arizona and Mexico, revere deer as the bringers of fruitfulness, cures and water, blessings invoked by deer-dancers.

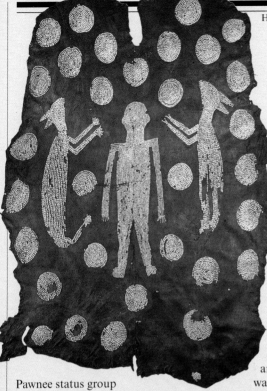

On this leather mantle decorated with shell beads, a deer (right) and a big cat, possibly guardian animal spirits, flank the figure of a man. The mantle is said to have once belonged to the 17th-century chief Powhatan (see p.33).

another doctor filled a sacred pipe and smoked to the animals. They then sent for immediate kin to bring meat to the lodge, where they carried out a secret ceremony to purify the beaver. Four days later, there began a complex ceremony in which the doctors smoked to the animals and symbolically breathed life into them. Each doctor prayed: "Now, father, I am poor; take pity upon me. I want your help to cure the sick. Keep sickness from our village. Give me good gifts and long life." If the animals were properly honoured, the supplication would be answered.

Pawnee status group after chiefs and priests. In January, when the animals began to stir, the keeper of the White Beaver prepared an altar and fireplace in his lodge. He and

HUNTING WITH REVERENCE

Subarctic and Arctic hunters follow stringent codes of respect toward their prey. At a feast after a hunt, the Mistassini Cree place food in the cooking fire so that the dead animals' spirits can eat from the smoke. Bears are especially sensitive. The bones of a butchered bear must be placed on a raised platform to keep scavengers away. If a bear finds out that its remains have been poorly treated, the offender and his family will suffer. Some Inuit believed that when a caribou had been killed, its head must be cut off at once to end the suffering of its soul. Whale hunters keep their camps neat and clean out of respect for their quarry, which is believed to appreciate tidiness.

The ivory seal and polar bear charms on these handles for Inuit draglines (straps used to haul dead animals) were said to win the animals' favour and bring the hunter luck.

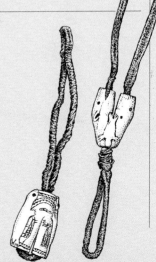

Plant rituals

For most peoples, plants provided more food than could be obtained from hunting and were revered as the gifts of Mother Earth. Some Indian nations had special relationships with particular plants, such as cultivated corn (maize), which people depended on for sustenance and which in turn depended on human farmers for its existence.

The first domesticated plants, such as sunflower, marsh elder and amaranth, were cultivated in temperate regions along rivers and in villages, where the disturbed nitrogen-rich soil to which they are ideally suited was to be found. Maize, the most important North American domesticate, was being cultivated in Central America by c.6000BC, and by c.AD1000 it was grown as far north as southern Canada, wherever the number of frost-free days and the amount of rainfall would allow. Maize supported 30,000 people in the prehistoric city of Cahokia (see pp.18–19), and the plant was of central importance

to the cosmology and ceremonial life of most groups for whom it was the principal crop. For example, the figure of Mother Corn played a focal role in Arikara origin myths. Other peoples for whom maize was prominent were the Mandan and the Pawnee on the Plains and the Choctaw in the Southeast.

The lifestyle of Great Basin peoples such as the Washo was centred on gathering the plants that sustained them (see pp.50–51). They lived in one of the drier regions of western North America and every year had to collect a store of seeds, roots and nuts to see them through the winter. Families would travel almost constantly to obtain a sufficient supply of the abundant but widely dispersed plants. The skills of locating and processing certain plants were handed down from mother to daughter, and thus the Washo women assumed great importance at gathering time. Most seeds had to be husked, winnowed and ground into flour, and

certain nuts, such as acorns, had to be leached to remove harmful ingredients. The need to gather food meant that the Washo lived in small scattered bands for much of the year. However, they came together in the autumn to harvest pinyon, a name given to any species of pine bearing edible nuts. Pine nuts provided a bounty beyond that of other plants, and the pinyon harvests, or *gumsaba*, were times of great ritual and sociability.

Native North Americans used many wild plants in ceremonies and curing. People used sage for ritual purification, bathing in its smoke. The medicinal properties of several plants were widely exploited. Chewing certain roots helped to relieve sore throats and headaches, while teas made from the leaves of various plants eased indigestion. Tobacco, in both wild and cultivated forms, was commonly used in rituals.

CORN WOMEN

Women play a central role in many sacred corn (maize) ceremonies, and the creation of corn is often attributed to a female figure. For example, according to the Cherokee, the first woman, Selu ("Corn"), gave birth to the first corn after rubbing her stomach. Selu, who also produced the first green beans from her breasts, is commemorated in the Green Corn Ceremony, in which she is represented by young women who carry baskets containing the first harvested plants of the year.

In the Southwest, the Zuni and a number of other Pueblo peoples ascribe the arrival of corn to beings known as the Six Corn Maidens. During the Hopi New Year celebrations at the time of the winter solstice, two *kachina* (spirit) sisters called Blue Corn Girl and Yellow Corn Girl participate in rituals to greet the return of the sun.

According to the Mandan, a being called Good Fur Robe organized the Goose Women Society, which handled many aspects of corn planting, care and harvesting, as well as various associated rituals. Goose Women were about 30 years old on average, but they could join the society at a much younger age. Members gradually worked their way up in rank. A person known as the Corn Priest oversaw their activities.

Goose Women organized dances throughout the corn-growing season. In spring and autumn, dances were linked to the migration of geese. The birds symbolized corn and were considered to be messengers of Old Woman Who Never Dies, who caused the grain to grow.

In this 20th-century painting, Cherokee women represent Selu, the first woman, during the Green Corn Ceremony.

World renewal

According to many Native North Americans, the rhythms of the universe are like those of a steady drumbeat, renewed and repeated only for as long as the drummer performs. In order to be renewed, the rhythms and cycles of nature also require human participation, in the form of rituals that mark important points in the cosmic cycle.

Many renewal rituals are held in spring and at other crucial times in the agricultural calendar. For example, the Tohono O'odham (Papago) of the Southwest hold a saguaro wine festival in June or July in order to prepare for the onset of the rainy season. The flesh of the harvested fruit (see p.55) is scooped into baskets, and the empty pods are left face up on the ground in order to encourage the spirits to fill them with rain. Some fruit is eaten raw, but the rest is boiled to produce a thick red syrup, which women seal in pots and then store. As it ferments, a male elder performs secret rites that are believed to turn the syrup into wine. The villagers gather a few days later to drink the wine during rainmaking ceremonies held to invoke the blessing of the first rains of the season.

The peoples of the Plains have a number of renewal ceremonies and practices, such as hoop dancing, in which a dancer manipulates several hoops to create shapes such as the sun, the moon, an eagle or a caterpillar, metamorphosing from one shape to the other with great skill. The hoops symbolize the eternal cycles of nature and the universal spirit that binds all things.

However, the principal renewal ceremony on the Plains is the annual Sun Dance. Held from late spring to early summer, its main purpose is to allow people to renew their faith in the spirits that guide the world. In the past, sun dancing was believed to guarantee a plentiful supply of buffalo in the coming year. For most Plains peoples, the Sun Dance is not a single performance, but a four-day cycle of rituals and sacred dances that relate to the forces of creation. Most dances are long ordeals that may involve self-torture. Dancers

A Canadian hoop dancer at Banff in Alberta. This hoop dance is being performed to honour the new growth of springtime.

fast and dance around a sacred tree for hours each day. On the last day, those dancers who have opted for self-torture are attached to the tree by thongs tied to skewers that are pushed through deep gashes in the flesh of their chest or back. They must endure this agony throughout the 24 songs of the dance, which takes several hours. At the climax of the dance, the exhausted dancers may attempt to pull themselves free of their bonds, ripping the skewers from their flesh as they do so. A dance is considered to be successful if a participant experiences a vision during his protracted ordeal.

THE SURVIVAL OF THE SUN DANCE

In the 19th century, white observers were shocked by the self-torture associated with the Sun Dance, and the practice was outlawed in 1881. This was a great blow to the Plains Indians, who believed that without this essential element the Sun Dance would not be effective and the world would not be renewed. In the following years, many Indians took to performing public Sun Dances for whites, simulating the piercing of the flesh by using harnesses. However, many other groups continued to hold traditional Sun Dances in secret, complete with the traditional piercing. Guards would be posted at a distance to warn of the approach of white officials.

Piercing was permitted again under the 1934 Indian Reorganization Act, but a full revival only took place in the 1960s with the growth of Indian militancy. Sun Dances take place today on most Plains reservations and in some urban areas where there are Indians of Plains origin.

A Cheyenne Sun Dance, by Indian artist Dick West. In a Sun Dance lodge, a dancer hangs by thongs fixed to his chest. Bison skulls attached to his back add to the weight pulling on the thongs.

Sacred History

Western anthropology uses the term "mythology" to refer to narratives that serve to explain the relationship between the natural and supernatural. However, Native North Americans prefer the phrase "sacred history", because of the popular notion that "myth" implies "fiction". For many Indians, the stories that relate the history of the earth, the origin of the people and the lives of the ancestors and sacred beings are very real. These figures and the great events of their times have left their enduring marks on the landscape, and they are vividly remembered in painted and carved images and in songs, dances and stories.

For some peoples, the earth was created in the union of cosmic giants; for others, it was brought up from the depths of an endless ocean by a small animal. Accounts of the struggles of the first people often tell of great heroes – supernatural beings that often took animal form. They helped the people on the long and arduous journey to their homeland from their place of origin, or brought them light and fire, or protected them from the wrath of destroyers. Danger also lurked in the form of unpredictable tricksters, who caused trouble with their mischief, but also helped to create the world as it is today.

Sam Kills Two, a Brule Dakota artist, adds another image to a "winter count" to represent the most notable event of the past year (see p.124). The photograph was taken in 1926, when this method of keeping annual records was already dying out among Plains peoples. The images on the count include sacred beings as well as real people and animals: many Native traditions do not distinguish between what Westerners regard as "real" and "mythical" history.

Creation stories

Native North American accounts of how the world came into being are dramas played out with characters and settings consistent with the environment in which the stories emerged. Creation stories include people and animals and also supernatural beings in human or animal form. Cosmic events draw upon such human experiences as sexual union, separation, dispute, great tests of strength and long, arduous journeys. The accounts are maintained by oral traditions, and Native holy people, storytellers and scholars recreate them at each telling, often incorporating new elements that have been acquired from dreams, visions and contemporary experience. In the last five centuries, the teachings of Christianity and pan-Indian religious movements have also been influential. They have brought to bear their own powerful metaphors about the beginnings of the world.

In some narratives, the world is created in a featureless void by gods. In Apache accounts, Black Wind made the earth and Yellow Wind gave it light, and a host of other gods contributed features of the landscape and forms of life. Other peoples believe that the world has always existed, but that in the beginning it was a flat, featureless plain, shrouded in darkness until the intervention of a great spirit. For the Shasta of California, Chareya (Old Man Above), who lived in the sky world, bored a hole in the sky and climbed down to the earth on a pile of ice and snow that he pushed through the hole. The sun shone through the hole and melted the ice, creating the sea, lakes and rivers. Chareya planted trees, and from their leaves he created birds. The Iroquoian origin myth also involves descent from the sky (see box, opposite).

Sex plays a role in some origin stories. For example, one Inuit creation account describes how two men emerged from a great world flood and lived together as man and wife. After the "wife" man became pregnant, his penis split and he turned into a woman, then gave birth to the first child.

Many Native North Americans today view the earth as a living essence personified as Mother Earth. For most tribes this is probably a quite recent concept (that is, post-contact with Europeans; see p.78), but for others it is a genuinely ancient tradition. For example, Salish-speaking peoples in the interior of British Columbia relate that a great spirit, Old One, made the earth out of a woman. This woman lies spread out on her back and people live on her. The trees and grass are her hair, the soil is her flesh, the rocks are her bones and the wind is her breath. When she feels cold, winter comes, and when she feels hot, it is summer. When she moves, there is an earthquake.

Indians have traditionally looked to the landscape and animals for clues to the sacred images, voices and events of the time when things came into being. Familiar animals are often said to play a crucial role in the creation process – for example, in the many stories that feature an "earthdiver". The earthdiver myth is a heroic creation story found in different forms all over the world. In many Native North American versions, the earth begins as an endless watery chaos with no dry land. A being asks various animals to dive to the bottom of this ocean to bring up mud. Eventually, one

MUSKRAT THE EARTHDIVER

A number of peoples ascribe the role of earthdiver to a muskrat. The following Beaver Indian account demonstrates the fluidity of the oral tradition, in contrast to versions that have been "tidied up" for non-Indian readers, such as the Iroquois tale recounted below. The Beaver tale was related in 1968 by Peter Chepesia of Prophet River Reserve in British Columbia. God asked Beaver to dive for soil. Beaver failed, so God asked Muskrat:

"Now Muskrat dive and he been gone for a long time, you know. So deep, you know. I don't think he get to the bottom right away. Was gone for a long time. They waiting up on top. And finally that Muskrat came back. He got a little dirt on his hand. You know. The little earth on his hand. He came back up, up on top and gave it to that God ... even now them, some of them guys say that Muskrat make the world for us. That's how it's made."

According to the Iroquoian earthdiver story, there was once

The sky woman falls through a hole in the sky world, in this depiction of the Iroquois creation myth by Ernest Smith, a Seneca artist. The turtle and the muskrat swim in the vast ocean below.

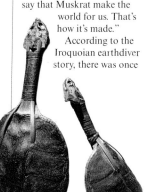

Turtle rattles such as these are used in curing rituals by the Iroquois False Face Society (see p.84) in honour of the turtle which carries the earth.

no earth, only an endless sea. People lived in a sky world above this one, where there was a great sacred tree. After the sky chief's wife dreamed that the tree was uprooted, the chief heaved it out, leaving a hole where the roots had been. The woman fell through the hole to the world below. Two swans caught her, but there was no place to put her down. Several birds and animals took turns to retrieve soil from the bottom of the sea. They all failed, but then the muskrat tried, and when it floated back to the surface, almost dead, it had a little mud in its paw. A turtle took the mud on its back, and the soil grew into a new world, upon which the swans gently let the sky woman down.

creature succeeds, and the dry land is formed from the mud it has retrieved. These animals are called "earthdivers" and are sometimes small and unassuming heroes. For example, in the Cherokee account the earthdiver is a water-beetle, while the Chickasaw say it is a crawfish and the Cheyenne a coot.

Earthdiver stories are most often told by hunting and gathering peoples, who draw upon their rich and profound relationship with the creatures of the woods, deserts or grasslands. Some farming groups, such as the Iroquois, also share this tradition, which suggests that the story predates their adoption of an agricultural way of life.

Other creation stories relate how the first people emerged from the ground, as crops do. Such accounts are more common among agricultural peoples, for example, the Pueblo peoples of the Southwest. In these myths, the struggle for existence often takes the form of a great migration through a number of worlds until the present world is

THE FOUR WORLDS

The Navajo story of creation tells of an upward migration through three worlds. The dark First World was the home of Begochiddy, First Man, First Woman, Salt Woman, Fire God and Coyote. Begochiddy, child of the sun, created insects, plants and five mountains. The six beings tired of this world and climbed the stem of a reed into a Second World, where Begochiddy created more mountains, clouds, plants and various life forms. Conflicts with other beings forced the six to climb the reed into a Third World, which had light, rivers, springs and abundant life.

Begochiddy created human beings, but evil magic caused men and women to fight, and Coyote stole the child of the Water Monster, who angrily caused a great flood. Again, the group climbed the reed, but it did not quite reach the next world. However, with the help of the Spider People and Locust, Begochiddy finally arrived in the Fourth World – this one – and found that it was an island in a vast sea. Four gods caused the waters to recede and winds dried the land. Begochiddy then created the world as the Navajo know it today.

This Navajo sandpainting, used in the Blessingway curing rituals, depicts various creator beings, including First Man, First Woman and Coyote.

The great kiva at Chetro Ketl, one of the ancient Anasazi pueblos in Chaco Canyon, New Mexico (see pp.56–7). To this day, kivas are the focus of the traditional ritual life of the Hopi and other Pueblo peoples of the Southwest. In Hopi kivas, a recess in the floor called the sipapu *commemorates the hole through which the first people emerged into the present world, according to the Hopi origin story (see pp.16–17).*

reached. In the Caddo origin story, the first man, Moon, is said to have created thousands of people in a single village in a world of darkness. With the help of a trickster, Coyote, he led them up through a hole into the present world. Many of them went astray on the journey to the Caddo homeland and these people were the ancestors of other Indian tribes. Those who remained with Moon established their homeland in a place called Tall-Timber-on-Top-of-the-Hill, where, with the help of Moon, Coyote and other beings, they gradually developed into the Caddo tribe. Over time, the speech of those who had strayed developed into different tongues, but originally the first people had all spoken Caddoan.

For most Native North Americans, the landscape preserves the memory of these great events so that the people may always be reminded of their iden-

tity. The Tewa world, for example, is enclosed by four sacred mountains and four sacred hills, in the centre of which is the hole whence the people are said to have emerged. For the Hopi, the sacred place of emergence is represented in every kiva (ceremonial chamber) as a hole in the floor.

This cedarwood carving by the modern Haida sculptor Bill Reid illustrates the moment in the Haida origin story when the first people began to crawl out of a clamshell that was found on the seashore by the creator-hero Raven.

Culture heroes

The mysterious creator beings who made the cosmos out of nothing are only very vaguely described in most Native North American oral traditions. They fashioned an empty, featureless world in which the drama of life subsequently unfolded and developed. Once the world had come into existence, beings who are altogether more familiar and accessible transformed the barren earth and made it habitable. Such characters are referred to by Western anthropologists as "culture heroes" or "transformers", and often possess human or animal personalities and characteristics. They gave the landscape its physical features and natural life, and defended the first people against monsters. They moved in and out of human affairs, bringing people light and fire and the tools and technologies of their traditional cultures.

Some of these transformers were unselfish and heroic, and adopted the role of guardians to ensure the survival of the first people and their descendants. For example, in one story told by the Penobscot of the Northeast, the hero Glúskap killed a monster frog who caused drought by drinking all the world's water. Among northern Athapaskan peoples, there is a hero widely known as Beaver Man (or, in some groups, as Old Man, Wise One or Navigator), who fought a number of fierce giants – Bear, Wolverine and others – who wanted to devour the first humans. These monsters tried to trap Beaver Man, but he always eluded them.

Other transformers were "tricksters" – unpredictable, selfish and mischievous personalities who often brought about changes to the world through the recklessness of their activities. For example, in Northwest Coast stories, the trickster Mink constantly brought trouble on himself as a result of his voracious sexual appetite. However, most of the transformers in Native traditions – Raven, Coyote, Cottontail and many others – possessed both heroic and trickster-like attributes.

According to Native North American belief, these beings lived in a sacred past that is not a remote, primordial period but a living, invisible world (see pp.12–13). This is a difficult concept for Westerners to grasp: it means that although events described in myths such as the Tsimshian story of Raven's theft of the moon (see p.123) happened in linear sequence, they have not receded into the past but exist still – together with Raven himself – "out there".

This "present past" is a world in which animals and people live in societies that are similarly structured. They can converse with each other and exchange forms at will. For example, the Raven in some Tsimshian stories is a man (or man-like being) who wears raven clothes, which he can take off to reveal his human form. Some Apache versions of the widespread hero-trickster Coyote wear Apache dress, speak and act like human beings, but also sometimes run around on all fours. It is only in the visible world that humans and animals have distinctive, fixed forms.

Indians perceive the evidence of this "present past" in visions and dreams and in the memories retained in oral tradition. The beings of this time often continue to make their presence felt in the physical

WINDIGO

Many North American Indian peoples tell stories of the fearsome creatures who can bring harm and death, and are often vanquished by culture heroes. The Northern Ojibway and Cree tell of giant cannibal ice-monsters known as windigos. A human could turn into a windigo after being driven to eat human flesh through starvation – an occasional but very real hazard even in the game-filled northern forests. To kill a real windigo was considered a truly heroic act, although spirits often came to the hero's assistance. The windigo had bulging eyes and long, pointed teeth, and became taller than the tallest trees when it shouted.

A windigo chased hunters on their solitary pursuit of moose and other game. Hunters who did not return to their camps were assumed to have fallen victim to a windigo's insatiable lust for human flesh. A windigo might stalk the woods disguised as an Indian, and any stranger who came to the village would be observed very carefully in case he was a windigo.

Windigo stories are very popular and are told for entertainment, like ghost stories among non-Indians. Sometimes they are told to enforce discipline among unruly children. Indian children once played a form of hide-and-seek in which a pretend windigo covered his head with leaves and hid.

Windigo *(1963), by the modern Anishinabe (Ojibway) artist Norval Morrisseau (born c.1933). In the windigo story illustrated here, the ice-hearted cannibal monster is eating beavers in the belief that they are human beings.*

The Thunderbird, lord of the skies and bringer of storms and rain, is depicted on this 19th-century Clayoquot dance robe from the Northwest Coast. Thunderbird features in many Native traditions as a culture hero – for example, killing dragon-like water beasts or catching whales to feed hungry people.

world. For example, every time there is a thunderstorm, a traditional Native North American may perceive the lightning as the flashing eyes of a being called the Thunderbird, and the wind as the roar of its huge wings.

The stories of heroes and tricksters are kept alive through the spoken word. Narratives are recounted in both religious and secular settings, and although they tell of a sacred time, they by no means constitute an inflexible liturgy that is rigid in form and content. Versions may differ substantially in detail. Sometimes two almost

wholly different myths may account for the same phenomenon. One story told by the Washo of California recounts that a figure called Creation Woman made the tribes of California out of cattail seeds. However, another Washo story says that the ancestors of the California peoples were the three quarrelling sons of Creation Man.

The flexibility and adaptability of Native mythology has allowed powerful external influences, such as Christianity, to introduce new characters into the old stories. For example, early in the 20th century, on the Northwest Coast, some trickster and transformer stories of the Salish people began to include a hero called Jesus the Traveller. He made fish out of fish bones and showed the people how to fashion axes, hammers and salmon traps.

Ancient traditions may have been weakened by external influences, but this has not prevented the appearance of new culture heroes of Native origin. These may be real people – Indians perceive no distinction between what a European would categorize as "mythical" and "historical". One recent culture hero is Dull Knife, a chief of the Northern Cheyenne. In defiance of his people's relocation to Oklahoma in 1877, Dull Knife led 383 ill and poorly-armed Cheyenne back to their homeland. He eluded the US Army until late October 1878, when he and his followers surrendered. They were incarcerated in an old barracks at Fort Robinson, Nebraska, from where Dull Knife led a spectacular breakout on 9 January 1879. Many of the Cheyenne were later killed, but Dull Knife, his family and others survived, and were eventually granted a reservation on the Tongue River in Montana. Dull Knife is remembered vividly by the modern Northern Cheyenne as the saviour of his nation. His triumphs are considered as magical and important as those of Coyote, Raven and other heroes who defied the enemies of the people.

RAVEN BRINGS LIGHT

Trickster heroes were valuable to humankind when they directed their mischief toward other supernatural beings. In one Tsimshian account, Txamsem (Raven) tricks a great sky chief out of his prized possession, the moon, so that the world's people, who until then have lived in a kind of eternal dusk, acquire light (the moon is understood to be the source of all light). In a version of this story, Raven turned himself into a pine-needle at a waterhole where the sky chief's daughter was drinking. She swallowed the needle, became pregnant and gave birth to Raven in the form of a child. Raven joined the sky chief's family and cajoled the chief into letting him play with a bladder ball – the container in which the moon was kept. One day, the family forgot to keep an eye on the child. He bounced the ball out of the door, changed into his old Raven clothes and flew back to the world of humans with the bladder.

Later, Raven asked a group of ghost people to give him some of the fish that they had just caught. They refused, and Raven angrily burst the bladder, because he knew how much all ghost people hated the light. As the bladder split, the moon was released and light flooded the skies. This was the first dawn.

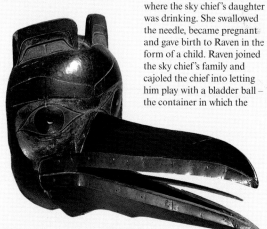

The hero-trickster Raven, portrayed here in a Haida mask, appears in many Native tales of the Northwest Coast. One story relates that Raven was originally white but was scorched black in the course of stealing fire for humankind.

Recording history

The peoples of North America had no writing and most history was orally transmitted by storytellers who used mnemonics to help them recall often complex details. However, this does not mean that Indians had no way of recording historical events. For example, many Plains groups possessed a type of permanent record known as the "winter count". Every year, usually in the winter, a symbol or realistic figure would be painted on a large, specially processed buffalo hide in order to commemorate the most signficant event affecting the community that year (see pp.114–15). The Kiowa Set-t'an calendar for 1882, for example, documents the efforts of a holy man, Pa-tepte, to bring back the herds of buffalo, which at that time were rapidly disappearing from the Plains (see pp.29 and 48). The calendar shows the figure of a medicine man seated in his sacred lodge, wearing a ceremonial red blanket trimmed with eagle feathers, with a buffalo beside him.

The organization of images on the winter count varied, but they were often arranged in a spiral, with the earliest picture in the centre. Some hides cover more than 200 years of tribal history. Few hides recorded any continuous series of events, and a winter count would be kept up only for as long as people were able to recount the events that it depicted.

In the Southwest, the Maricopa, Pima and Tohono O'odham (Papago) would mark the passage of time by carving annual symbols on the flattened side of "calendar sticks" – strips of wood a yard (0.9m) or so long. Each symbol stood for an event that distinguished a particular year, which would

STORYTELLING

Traditionally, the storyteller is a highly valued member of Native North American society. In many groups, the audience is required to give the teller some gift in exchange for a story – perhaps tobacco or meat, or another food item. Storytelling may be accompanied by certain formalities: among the Maidu, for example, listeners were asked to lie on their backs to stay more attentive. Cheyenne storytellers had first to smooth the ground

The Story Teller, a modern pottery sculpture from Jemez Pueblo, New Mexico.

and then brush their bodies with their hands. Sometimes chants or prayers in a language that the audience could not understand would precede the story.

Stories had traditional opening formulas, rather like the "once upon a time" of English tales. Seneca stories might begin with "When the world was new", and Zuni ones with "Now we are taking it up". The actions of storytellers also varied. Some remained seated, using only the inflection of their voice to carry emotional content. Others would play the part of characters in their story, using a combination of voice, motion and gesture.

be recalled by a "calendar stick keeper", a specialist who had the same status as curers, singers and potters. A new symbol was carved around the time of the summer harvest of the saguaro cactus each year. Keepers from different communities shared their knowledge – this enabled them to keep in touch with events that took place outside their immediate community. The sticks were accurate enough to allow senior members of the tribe to know their own birthdays precisely. Like the winter counts, however, the sticks depended on the memories of individuals for their usefulness as historical documents. On the death of the keepers, they might be sold, but they were often destroyed.

In the Northeast, important events were often recorded in belts of wampum (beads made from seashells). Wampum-keepers would memorize the details of the event commemorated. Wampum belts were used as records of treaties, such as that which founded the Iroquois League (see p.41).

The Lenni Lenape (Delaware) people of the Northeast maintained a pictorial historical record known as the Walum Olum. Painted on bark, it contained more detail than other records, but still relied on the memory of a skilled storyteller. The events depicted on it were recounted at ceremonial storytellings that could last for weeks and involved a major feat of memory on the part of the teller. One surviving fragment deals with the period of contact with Europeans, starting c.1600 and ending c.1818.

This wampum belt was presented to the French by the Huron in 1611. The belt represented a formal request for an alliance.

The Survival of the Sacred

For Native North Americans, the disruption wrought by Europeans and their American successors was violent, far-reaching and often very sudden. Within less than a generation, a people's way of life could change radically. New diseases decimated populations. Forced relocation disrupted family life and shifted groups to landscapes with which they were unfamiliar and which did not feature in their sacred stories. Displacement led to confrontation not only with whites, but also between Indian groups who were thrown together and forced to compete for ever more meagre resources. The eradication of the buffalo by white hunters destroyed the subsistence base for dozens of peoples.

In these adverse circumstances, Indians tried to hold on to their traditional ways of life for as long as possible. But change was inevitable if Indian groups were ever to adjust to the new situation and survive as distinct cultural entities. New, pan-Indian religious movements arose, some of them millennarian, predicting the end of the white ascendancy and the return of the old ways. Other spiritual movements saw survival in terms of a continuation of the intimate relationship between people, nature and spirit that was the underlying essence of many Native cultures.

Worshippers gather in firelit tipis for a ritual of the Native American Church, a spiritual revival movement that became widespread from the late 19th century (see p.131).

Keeping traditional ways

In spite of the many changes that have beset Indian peoples since the arrival of the first white settlers, their core beliefs have remained firm. In essence, these are that a Creator ordained the laws of nature and the ways of the sacred, which are immutable. As one Southern Cheyenne woman, Viola Hatch, has recently put it: "We do not have a set of guidelines written on a piece of paper to show us how to live. We got it from the Great Spirit. He told us one time, we learned it, followed it to this day." It is believed that although people's material circumstances may alter, the sacred cycles of nature will continue as before, and the sacred past will always be close at hand (see pp.12–13). No amount of upheaval and human interference can alter the most important elements of Native life: one's people, one's family and one's sacred relationships with the animal, plant and spirit worlds. As the Lakota elder Matthew King (see p.80) has said: "We have been here for millions of years. God gave us ... laws to govern our people. We cannot change [them]. No one can change [them]. We cannot make laws."

The oral tradition is central to the survival of Native North American ways. One generation passes ancient stories on to the next as a way of teaching traditional morality and history, and the correct way of performing the ancient rituals and ceremonies that punctuate the year. The importance of maintaining the oral tradition is that it prevents ancient stories from becoming fossilized, a tendency whenever sacred narratives are written down. Details of a story will change to reflect new circumstances in the life of the people.

Luminarias (bonfires) light up Taos Pueblo, New Mexico, on Christmas Eve. They form part of traditional midwinter ceremonies that date back to pre-Christian times.

THE RETURN OF THE AHAYU:DA

In recent years, many Indian peoples have sought the return of sacred objects from museums as part of their attempt to ensure the survival of Native traditions. One campaign ended in March 1987, when the Zuni of New Mexico celebrated the return of wooden images of the Ahayu:da, the twin gods or war gods, that had been removed to the Smithsonian Institution in the 1880s. Every two years, at the winter solstice, holy men place such images in shrines overlooking Zuni Pueblo as part of a ritual to invoke the protection of the deities. The Zuni called for the return of the effigies in 1978. Negotiations with the Smithsonian were protracted, but as Indian efforts to repatriate sacred objects accelerated nationally, the museum relented. Other US museums are now also returning Ahayu:da effigies to the Zuni. (See also pp.144–5.)

Sacred objects, such as those kept in sacred bundles (see p.84), also contribute to the maintenance of traditional ways. Bundles may contain items that are said to go back to the first people, and they may thus encapsulate the entire history of a clan. Personal "medicine bundles" remind the owner of his or her personal relationship with the spirit world, as revealed in visions or dreams. A Crow man who had dreamed of a beaver would make a medicine bundle from beaver skin, and put in it rocks, beads and animal parts that he perceived to be a source of personal "medicine" (spirit power).

Like the details of ancient orally-transmitted stories, the contents of a sacred bundle may be renewed periodically. Objects in personal bundles are added or removed as the owner has new spiritual revelations. This openness to change, above all, has ensured that the most ancient traditions have remained relevant to Native North Americans in the modern world (see also pp.156–7).

Dreams

Dreams and visions are of great significance in most Indian traditions, and have proved important in helping Native peoples to confront the challenge of white intrusion. Dreaming is believed to be a source of spirit power, which may be used to gain knowledge and insight or to foretell the future. For example, the Athapaskan-speaking Beaver Indians of the Peace River in British Columbia and Alberta believed that even the dreams of a small child had significance, but the most important dreams occurred when a person had been on a vision quest and made a personal "medicine bundle" (see p.129). The medicine bundle would be hung behind the place where its owner slept and was believed to exert a powerful influence over his or her dreams.

Individuals sometimes dreamed of songs that became their personal possessions, and of personal taboos forbidding certain foods or activities. A dream could also be used as a defence against witchcraft, and prophets could dream of future events. Dreams usually require interpretation by an elder or a holy person, who can help the dreamer to understand their significance.

It is not always easy to distinguish dreams from visionary experiences that occur during unconscious states other than sleep. For example, it is difficult to know whether what Black Elk described (see opposite page) was really a dream or a vision during a coma caused by illness. Sometimes, an individual may experience a "dream" after embarking on a vision quest (see p.99).

A dream may relate to the daily life of an individual, but sometimes can give access to matters of great importance for a whole people. In the wake of the physical and moral devastation inflicted by whites on Native ways of life, dreams inspired a number of movements that sought to revive Indian morale and to find genuinely Indian ways of coping with a radically changed world. This was the case with the great dream-visions of the Seneca prophet Handsome Lake (see pp.132–4) and others. During such prophetic visions, the dreamer is often said to travel outside his or her body to worlds beyond human society, on spiritual journeys full of symbolic images.

This drawing of c.1890 by Walter Bone Shirt, a Lakota Sioux, shows a scene from a Buffalo Society dance. Members of the society were believed to receive messages from the spirit of the buffalo through dreams. They held special dances to honour the animal, during which a holy man appeared in a buffalo headdress, as shown here. As he danced, he was stalked by a young man who assumed the role of a Lakota hunter.

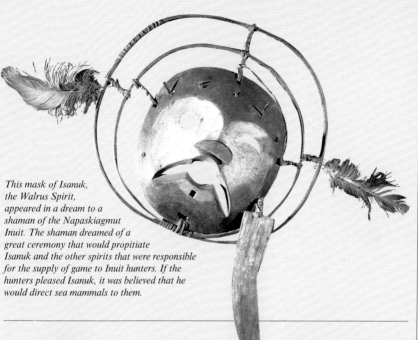

This mask of Isanuk, the Walrus Spirit, appeared in a dream to a shaman of the Napaskiagmut Inuit. The shaman dreamed of a great ceremony that would propitiate Isanuk and the other spirits that were responsible for the supply of game to Inuit hunters. If the hunters pleased Isanuk, it was believed that he would direct sea mammals to them.

Black Elk, aged about 82.

BLACK ELK

Owing to the popularity of John Neihardt's book *Black Elk Speaks*, published in 1923, the holy man Black Elk (1864–1950) is probably the best-known Native North American dream visionary of recent times. He lived at a crucial period for the Oglala Sioux people, the beginning of conflict with whites that would lead to defeat in the Indian Wars and the beginning of reservation life. Black Elk was instrumental in the establishment of the Ghost Dance (see pp. 136–7), and worked for his people's survival until his death. According to Neihardt's book, when Black Elk was nine years old, in 1873, he lapsed into unconsciousness for 12 days. During this period, he experienced a great dream-vision in which two men led him up to the clouds. They showed him a bay horse called the "Horse of the Four Directions" (north, east, south and west). The animal led him to a cloud, where he saw his six "grandfathers" – ancestral figures who embodied the six directions (north, east, south, west, up and down). Each of the six told Black Elk of important powers that would make him a holy man who could cure and settle strife. They gave him the task of leading the people back to the sacred Red Road, the Indian way (see p. 156), as a way to ensure their survival. Black Elk is said to have beheld many wonders that enabled his people to cope with the coming white onslaught.

Nativistic movements

Many spiritual movements arose to help Indians to come to terms with the upheaval caused by the arrival of whites. Anthropologists refer to such movements as "nativistic" – meaning that they represent an attempt by native peoples to ensure the survival, in whatever form proves necessary, of aboriginal culture in the face of pressure to assimilate. North American nativistic movements aimed to reaffirm Native North American values where altered conditions may have rendered traditional ceremonies – such as those celebrating a landscape where the people no longer lived – meaningless or incongruous.

There were two types of nativistic movement: "revitalization" and "millennarian". Both were syncretic – in other words, they adopted some of the beliefs and practices of the dominant culture – but to different degrees. In the first type, Indians were able to defuse much white criticism of their values by adopting some Christian forms and symbols and eliminating traditional elements that the missionaries denounced as heathen, satanic or superstitious. Some revitalization movements, such as the Handsome Lake Movement and the Native American Church (see box, opposite), took congregational forms

Handsome Lake preaching in the tribal longhouse on the Tonawanda Reservation, by the 20th-century Seneca artist Ernest Smith. Handsome Lake, a holy man of great repute, had his famous dream when he was 64 and had himself fallen victim to the alcohol abuse that afflicted his people. About a quarter of the Iroquois had become followers of his teaching by the middle of the 19th century.

THE NATIVE AMERICAN CHURCH

Among the most important revitalization movements is the Native American Church, sometimes derogatorily called the Peyote Cult. With about 250,000 members, it is also a pan-Indian movement.

Originating in Mexico, the church initially spread across the Plains after the collapse of the Ghost Dance. It has since become popular in the Midwest and Southeast. Church members seek visions by eating parts of the round, mildly hallucinogenic peyote cactus as a sacrament during

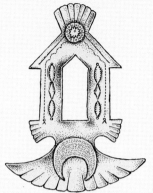

A peyote and a crescent altar used in meetings are among Native American Church symbols on this tie-slide.

church meetings. Led by a "peyote chief" or "roadman" who travels between groups,

meetings are held in a tipi from dusk to dawn and involve rattles, bone whistles and other traditional elements. Church doctrine is a mixture of Christianity and traditional belief. God is a great spirit and Jesus is a guardian spirit. The ideal of brotherly love and some of the Ten Commandments are among core beliefs. Members do not drink alcohol.

Despite its strictly sacramental use, peyote was outlawed for a time. Its use by the Native American Church is now largely recognized, but many whites still fight to ban it.

---

similar to those of the Christian churches. Such movements allowed a core of traditional belief to survive almost by camouflage within the trappings of Christianity.

The second, and generally more confrontational, type of nativistic movement is called "millennarian". Such movements arose when subjugation by whites was so rapid that traditional culture was in danger of immediate collapse. Revitalization movements were sometimes, but not necessarily, headed by prophetic figures. Millennarian movements, however, almost always began with a prophet preaching an imminent, sometimes cataclysmic end to the current order and a return to traditional ways.

Some scholars suggest that Indian nativistic prophets arose as a result of contact with the Christian prophetic tradition. Millennarian movements in particular appear to have been inspired by Jesus' call for the Jews to return to

their traditional values, and his promise that God would sweep away the current order and establish a spiritual kingdom that would last a millennium (hence the term "millennarian"). However, other scholars argue that Native prophets had their roots in a type of pre-contact ceremony called a "Prophet Dance", a communal dance at which prophesying, exhortations and trances occurred. Whatever the case, the Native prophets were innovators, willing to bring new beliefs and practices to their people.

Prophets usually arose in the worst of circumstances, such as those which beset the Seneca before the rise of Handsome Lake. Many were holy people, such as the Paiute prophet Wodziwob (see pp.136–7). Other prophets had no sacred training at all, but possessed oratorical or political skills. Most became prophets as a result of personal visions or dreams.

The first great revitalization movement, the Handsome Lake Movement, or Longhouse Religion, arose in the Northeast. This syncretic movement began in 1799 among the Seneca, a people of the Iroquois League (see p.41). After the American Revolution (1775–83), in which the Seneca had sided with Britain, Seneca lands were confiscated, sold or stolen. Food became scarce and alcoholism hastened the threat of social collapse. It was at this point that Handsome Lake, the brother of a chief, dreamed of an encounter with spirits, who advised the Seneca to give up alcohol and all dancing except a "Worship Dance". They also advised peaceful accommodation with whites. Handsome Lake's vision included a heaven and hell for Indians alone. Those who believed in his "Good Message" met for weekly worship in a longhouse. The religion was very successful among the Six Nations and is practised to this day.

Other movements came to the fore in the early 19th century, such as those of the Shawnee prophet (see below) and the Ojibway prophetess, a nameless, charismatic Ojibway woman who apparently visited the northern Columbia River region. She may have inspired the Wanapum prophet Smohalla, "The Preacher", who was among the best known prophets from the Northwest Coast. A holy man from the Columbia River valley, in 1860 he proclaimed a message that he said came from the land of the spirits. The essence of his prophecy was that the fortunes of the Indians would be restored if they refused to follow white

---

THE SHAWNEE PROPHET

During the early 1800s, Shawnee culture was nearing a crisis point. The people were in continual conflict with whites on the frontier, lands had been overhunted and disease and alcohol had taken a severe toll. In 1805, Lalawethika, the younger brother of the Shawnee chief Tecumseh, fell into a series of visionary trances during an epidemic. Previously a lazy, boastful drinker, he emerged from his visions a new man. He declared that the "Master of Life" had shown him a paradise full of game and fertile cornfields, as the Shawnee world had been before the arrival of the whites. If the Shawnee returned to the path of virtue, this paradise would return. Many of the virtues preached by Lalawethika, or Tenskwatawa ("Open Door"), as he now called himself, were

traditional Shawnee values, but others drew on Christian teachings. Tenskwatawa attracted many converts, including Tecumseh, most of whom were not Shawnee. By 1807, the brothers had established a settlement called Prophet's Town, and the US government began to see the movement as a threat. In 1811, against advice, the prophet engaged federal troops at Tippicanoe, outside the town. The Shawnee were routed and Tenskwatawa abruptly lost almost all his influence. Tecumseh took over from his brother until his own death in battle two years later.

Tenskwatawa, the Shawnee prophet, in a portrait of 1823 by Charles Bird King.

Bole-Maru dancers, photographed in 1907 by C. Hart Merriam. Individuals known as Dreamers, who were privy to messages from the Creator, conducted Bole-Maru rituals and assumed many traditional diagnostic and healing functions.

ways that "wounded" Mother Earth, such as mining and ploughing. Smohalla's prophecies became the foundation of many Ghost Dances of the Northwest Coast and Plains (see pp.136–7).

Smohalla also inspired several nativistic movements in California, where severe cultural disruption sparked a rapid succession of movements in the late 19th century. One of these, the Bole-Maru, combined traditional values with Christian-inspired dualistic ideas of heaven and hell, God and the Devil.

The Bole-Maru movement is still active among some Californian peoples, as is the Indian Shaker Church, which arose in the 1880s. Shakers claim to receive power directly from God during trances characterized by fits of trembling. The church emphasizes faith-healing using songs that combine Indian melodies and a mixture of traditional and Christian lyrics. Major ceremonies, which involve some traditional world renewal rituals (see pp.112–13), are held around Easter and in August.

The Ghost Dance

The most popular and widespread of all millennarian movements was the Ghost Dance, which started among the Paiutes. It was never a unified movement but a series of similar revitalization cults derived from one source. Common Ghost Dance features included a circle dance in which the dancers were said to visit dead relatives in a visionary trance.

In 1870, disease killed more than a tenth of the Paiute population. Shortly afterward, in Fish Lake valley in present-day Utah, a *wovoka*, or "weather doctor" – one said to possess powers over rain, earthquakes and other natural phenomena – dreamed that he was given the power to bring back the souls of those who had recently died. According to this dream, the people had to paint themselves and perform circle dances. The *wovoka* became known as Wodziwob, the Paiute term for an elder, a curer or a doctor. When the people rested from dancing, Wodziwob would fall into a trance, during which, he claimed, he visited the dead, who promised to return to their loved ones soon. News of Wodziwob spread into California, the Great Basin and the Plateau, largely through the work of Tavibo, another weather doctor. But the Paiute Ghost Dance came to an abrupt end in 1872, when Wodziwob declared that he had been tricked by an evil witch owl.

Ghost Dances were revived by Tavibo's son, who was also trained as a weather doctor and came to be known simply by this title (Wovoka). He worked on a Mormon ranch, received an English name, Jack Wilson, and learned about Christianity. On 1 January 1889, during an illness, Wovoka experienced a trance in which he claimed to visit the land of the dead, where God told him to preach peace. Wovoka said that Native people could meet the dead and visit the former world of traditional Indian ways during circle dances. He preached that Indians must not fight and could even adopt some white ways for the sake of peace.

Many Plains groups sent emissaries to Wovoka. Each group translated his message to meet its own needs. The Lakota version was more revolutionary than its model, and shows Christian influence. The Lakota said that Wovoka was the son of the Great Spirit, who had risen from the dead after being killed by

"The Larger Circle", a part of the Arapaho Ghost Dance. This painting by Mary I. Wright is based on a photograph taken by James Mooney in 1893 for the Smithsonian Institution.

whites. Eventually, all whites would be swept away in a fiery cloud, the dead and the bison would return, and a new world would come into being. Like other peoples, many Lakota wore special Ghost Dance shirts, which they believed would protect them from bullets.

The US Army used the spread of the Ghost Dance as an excuse to disarm any Plains Indian groups still seen as a potential threat. During one such operation, at Wounded Knee, South Dakota, in December 1890, nervous troops massacred 200 Lakota men, women and children. For Indians, Wounded Knee stands to this day as a monument to the white suppression not only of the Ghost Dance, but of Native culture in general.

A Pawnee Ghost Dance drum of c.1890, painted with an image of the Thunderbird (see p.122), a being whose powers were invoked in the dance.

A GHOST DANCE REVIVAL

In 1973, members of the American Indian Movement (AIM) occupied Wounded Knee for several weeks. The spiritual leader of the takeover, Lakota holy man Leonard Crow Dog (see p.98), had always believed that the Lakota emissaries to Wovoka had misunderstood his message. They should not have thought that they could bring back the dead, but should have seen the circle dance as a means of keeping traditional ways alive by creating a link with the past and the ancestors. During the protest, Crow Dog conducted a Ghost Dance in the place where it had died in 1890. Women worked throughout the night to make Ghost Dance shirts out of burlap and curtains, painting them in traditional ways. Many dancers wore American flags upside down, a common form of AIM protest.

Since 1973, Crow Dog has continued to practise the Ghost Dance on Crow Dog's Paradise, his family land on the Rosebud Reservation in South Dakota.

To the Seventh Generation

Seven is a number with great significance in the traditions of many Indian nations. For example, the Lakota speak of seven "origin people" and had Seven Council Fires. Seneca wisdom distinguishes "seven talents". The Pawnee used the position of the Seven Stars (known to Europeans as the Pleiades) to determine the beginning of the ceremonial year. Above all, many Native North Americans recognize a profound responsibility to those who will come after them, down to the Seventh Generation.

This means that a person's behaviour is guided by consideration for the future. Some Indians look to the future by keeping alive traditional themes in new, perhaps non-traditional ways – for example, by writing novels and plays, or through art. Others struggle to restore what they regard as the world's balance by demanding the return of the remains of ancestors and other ancient relics stored on museum shelves, and by reclaiming land illegally taken. Some strive to provide employment where it is needed, or to protect their culture by educating the young in their own traditions, while also giving them the tools that will enable them to compete in the modern world.

A Crow elder and two boys in traditional dress at the annual Crow Fair at Crow Agency, Montana, the centre of the Crow nation. The week-long fair includes powwow dancing, Indian games and other traditional events. Such festivals play a crucial role in reaffirming tribal identity and passing on Native traditions to the younger generation.

The drum is a circle

In Native North American philosophy, the roundness of a drum symbolizes the inseparable unity of the past, present and future. This unity is a circle that binds all people. The beating of the drum represents the eternal rhythms of nature. For Native North Americans, these rhythms are echoed in the speech of the traditional storyteller and the stories of the modern Indian writer.

Native North American oral traditions encompass a wide range of genres, from simple moral tales to powerful oratory. Contact with other cultures and the development of written Native languages have enabled Native peoples to expand their forms of expression even further. In recent times, the keen storytelling that is a feature of many Native cultures has provided a foundation for the growth of written creativity and the appearance of a Native North American literature. Native literature has not only served to keep Native traditions alive, but has also acted as a bridge between Native culture and mainstream white society.

The autobiographical tradition provides perhaps the most direct means of communicating the realities of Indian life to outsiders. The first book in which an Indian author translated the Native experience for non-Natives was probably *Son of the Forest* by William Apess, a mixed-blood Pequot of the Northeast. In this autobiography, which appeared in 1829, Apess wrote of the abuses he and other Indians had suffered at the hands of whites, and about his personal religious beliefs. Apess has been followed notably by Luther Standing Bear (Lakota), Charles Eastman (Santee Dakota), John Rogers (Ojibway) and Paula Gunn Allen (Laguna Pueblo). Biographical works have also been influential – for example, John Neihardt's *Black Elk Speaks* (1923), about the life of the Lakota visionary Black Elk (see p.131). However, the genuinely Indian character of this and other, similar works is doubtful. In such works, a non-Indian author has imposed a narrative structure that is not its subject's own and thus may lack authenticity.

The first novel written by a Native author was *Wynema* (1891) by Sophie Alice Callahan, a mixed-blood Creek. Her work addressed important tribal issues of her day, such as the Ghost Dance (see pp.136–7) and the massacre at Wounded Knee. The novel has proved a particularly fruitful genre for

Navajo children listen to stories told by an elder. The oral tradition remains central to the survival of Native languages and wisdom in modern North American society (see also p.124).

(Hopi–Miwok) and Maurice Kenny (Mohawk). A prominent theme of many North American Indian novelists is the problem of Native identity and how to cope with the dominant white culture.

Native poetry has more direct links with the oral tradition, and poets such as Gerald Vizenor and Joy Harjo (Creek) seek to capture the emotional intensity and rhythms of the spoken Native language. Contemporary poetry, like most Indian literature, is written in English, but nonetheless seeks to preserve the speech patterns, spirit and content of Native tongues.

The written word is important, but it has not displaced the oral tradition, which continues to thrive, both in English and Native languages, as a means of expressing ancient wisdoms and contemporary conditions. The written and the spoken genres have a shared goal: to record and to clarify the Native North American experience, which outsiders have often distorted or dismissed as being of no significance.

Native writers, several of whom have achieved wide acclaim, such as N. Scott Momaday (Kiowa), winner in 1968 of a Pulitzer Prize for *House Made of Dawn*. American Book Awards have gone to Louise Erdrich (Ojibway; see below), Gerald Vizenor (Ojibway), Wendy Rose

LOUISE ERDRICH

Among the best-known of contemporary Native North American novelists is Louise Erdrich, born in 1954 of an Ojibway mother and a father of German descent. Her works, many of which are set in the region of North Dakota where she grew up, have received critical praise both in the US and abroad. Erdrich explores some of the central issues facing modern Native North Americans, in particular the struggle to retain their Indian identity in the face of the almost overwhelming pressure to assimilate imposed by the dominant white culture. This problem, and the strain that it puts on relationships between and within the older and younger generations, forms the basis of Erdrich's acclaimed four-volume family saga consisting of *Love Medicine* (1984, the winner of the National Book Critics' Circle Award and the *Los Angeles Times* Book Award), *The Beet Queen* (1986), *Tracks* (1988) and *The Bingo Palace* (1993).

The drum is a heartbeat

Native dancers move to a drumbeat that, for Indians, symbolizes the human pulse and the fundamental rhythms of all life. For this reason, performance has always played an important part in Native expression, and both dance and music have undergone an extraordinary renaissance in recent years. Indian creativity has also found outlets in such non-traditional visual forms as the theatre and fine art. Indian artistic expression often relates to specific tribal concerns and heritage, but it also touches on pan-Indian themes. Many songs and dances are intertribal, and form part of the repertoire of such noted ensembles as the American Indian Dance Theater.

Native musicians – for example, R. Carlos Nakai and Kevin Locke – have received international acclaim for their flute playing, compositions and dancing. Many Native musicians have had success on the "New Age" music scene, but more genuinely traditional forms also thrive. For example, the Ihanktonwan Singers, a group of Yankton Sioux children aged seven to 14, perform widely in the northern Plains region.

Native theatre is also flourishing, especially in Canada, where Native Earth Performing Arts, the leading Canadian aboriginal theatre company, performs plays by noted Indian writers such as Joyce B. Joe and Tomson Highway (see box, opposite).

Each September, in Sioux Falls, South Dakota, the Northern Plains Tribal Arts Show draws artists from the entire region and thousands of visitors. On display are paintings and sculptures on Native themes, in a range of abstract and figurative styles. There is also work

in traditional media, and the show includes dance and music, from singers of old Indian songs to country-and-western and protest groups. The success of the arts show and the establishment of Native galleries across North America testify to the wide interest prompted by the Native artistic resurgence.

Comanche dancers Morgan Tosee and Gary Tolsah, members of the American Indian Dance Theater (AIDT), perform a spectacular Shield Dance. The AIDT is one of many combined Native North American dance and theatre groups. Other noted ensembles include the Naa Kahidi Theater of southeast Alaska. Both groups have performed widely in North America and abroad.

TOMSON HIGHWAY

Native North Americans have been depicted in the theatre in Canada since the early 17th century, when Marc Lescarbot produced entertainment for French colonists at Port Royale in present-day Nova Scotia. The stereotyping of Indians that characterized Lescarbot's productions of 1603 has been a feature of most other plays in which Native characters have appeared. For example, behind the sympathetic portrayal of a Native woman in George Ryga's 1970 play, *The Ecstasy of Rita Joe*, lay the common assumption that her culture was dying. However, since 1986, the works of a young Cree playwright, Tomson Highway, have sought to shatter the overworn illusions about Native people by presenting modern life as it is really lived on "the rez" (an Indian reserve).

Highway was born in 1951 in a tent along his father's trapline in northern Manitoba. He endured the common Native Canadian experience of having to be separated from his family and culture for most of the year at a boarding school. He graduated with an honours degree in music from the University of Western Ontario.

Highway's first play, *The Rez Sisters* (1986), was a fresh, earthy and vigorous examination of the lives of Native Canadian women on the fictional Wasaychigan Hill Reserve. The play was an instant success, winning major Canadian theatre awards and representing Canada at the Edinburgh International Festival. Highway's next play, *Dry Lips Oughta Move to Kapuskasing* (1989), was another frank examination of Native life – it dealt with the sensitive subject of male sexism on Indian reserves. He continues to write with warmth and sharp, ironic wit about his people, aiming to bring Native Canadians clearly and directly into the consciousness of mainstream white Canadian society.

The wider acceptance of Native North American theatre among non-Indians has been difficult to achieve. However, through the work of Highway and others, the voices of Native playwrights and actors are increasingly to be heard in mainstream theatre.

Reclaiming the past

As whites took over Native lands, white scholars became keen to study the nature and origins of the Indians, who many felt would soon disappear. In 1867, US Army personnel were ordered to obtain Indian skulls for study at the Army Medical Museum. Thousands of skulls were collected from battlefields and burial grounds. In the following decades, several important museums and universities collected skeletons and burial goods for study and display. Some private collectors looted graves and sold remains and funerary goods as curios, or exhibited them to tourists.

For Native North Americans, such actions are sacrilegious. Many traditional Indians believe that the dead continue to exist, but in a different world, and that the removal of their remains is an affront to the dignity of the ancestors and a threat to the delicate harmony of nature. For decades, Indians fought to have remains repatriated for reburial. Finally, in 1990, Congress passed the Native American Graves Protection and Repatriation Act (NAGPRA). Under this act, any organization associated

Native protesters on Alcatraz, the former island-prison in San Francisco Bay. Around 200 Indians occupied the island in November 1969, shortly after the US government had closed the prison. They demanded that the island be handed over to Indians, basing their claim on land treaty clauses that promised to return territory to Indians should it ever become surplus to federal requirements. The siege of Alcatraz lasted until 1971, when the last demonstrators were expelled by federal marshals. But other protests followed, including a march on Washington, D.C., in 1972 called "The Trail of Broken Treaties", during which the Bureau of Indian Affairs was occupied for six days.

CROW CREEK

The Crow Creek reburial provided a model for consultation between Indians and archaeologists on the issue of ancient graves. In 1978, University of South Dakota archaeologists at the ancient Crow Creek Village site on the Crow Creek Sioux Reservation discovered the bones of 500 victims of a massacre that took place c.AD1325 during warfare among ancestors of the Arikara. The Arikara and the Sioux were traditional enemies, but collaborated to secure the future of the remains. They insisted at first that the bones should not be touched, but when looters began to damage the site they agreed to let the bones be removed for study, as long as they were returned. In 1981, the bones were reburied close to where they had been found.

ABOVE, LEFT *Indian holy men pray at the site of the reburial, which was accompanied by Christian and traditional rites.* ABOVE *The bones as they were discovered in 1978.*

with the government must return all remains, grave goods and sacred objects to the peoples from which they were taken, and must consult with tribes directly before excavating any Indian sites.

Indians have had more mixed success in their struggle to regain lands that were lost by treaty or conquest. The legal fight began in 1946, when the US Congress set up the Indian Claims Commission (ICC). The ICC set compensation for illegally taken lands at the value of the land when it was seized, plus interest. This brought considerable financial gains to peoples whose claims were allowed. For example, the Passamaquoddy of Maine received enough money to develop housing, industry and education programmes. However, some peoples have refused to accept money on the grounds that the earth is sacred and cannot be bought and sold. The outcome of such cases is uncertain (see also p.161).

Unlike the US, Canada recognizes that Indians have rights based on traditional occupation. The government pursues comprehensive agreements that involve land deals and financial settlements. The most notable result of this policy has been the creation of the Inuit territory of Nunavut (see pp.163 and 170–71). However, as in the US, there are many unresolved cases.

Native scholars

Traditionally, Native people learned by listening to and watching their elders and then working with them in the tasks of daily life. Indian children sat at the feet of storytellers, whose tales of warriors and tricksters and other spirit beings served as lessons in morality, philosophy and religion. Later, as youths, they would begin to learn the responsibilities of adulthood, such as how to gather and prepare plants for food and medicine, to track and hunt, and to make the clothing and tools necessary for survival.

Schools put an end to this traditional way of learning. Reservation schools and boarding schools that separated children from their families for up to ten months a year (see p.25) attempted to assimilate Indian and Inuit people by disconnecting the children from their traditional culture. Indian education policies may be less harsh today, but almost all young Native North Americans still attend public (state) schools. Systematic, school-based learning is inconsistent with the more flexible and individually-oriented tribal method of learning. But the main problem is that the state school system reflects the heritage and values of the dominant white society, which often contradict traditional teachings. As a result, many Indians have left school ill-equipped to deal effectively with either their own culture or that of the dominant society.

To provide education that is more sensitive to Native traditions, groups such as the American Indian Movement (AIM) have sought in recent years to establish model schools for Indians. In 1971, in Minneapolis, AIM opened the first Native peoples survival school, which sought to help young Indians to adjust to white society without losing touch with their own culture. Native-

run elementary and secondary schools have blossomed since that time. In Native schools, curricula take into account traditional festivals and other events. For example, at the Nunamiut School in Anaktuvuk, Alaska, classes in October are organized around traditional Inuit activities associated with cranberry picking.

The problems encountered in Native schools also applied to tertiary education. There were no Native colleges before 1968, when the Navajo Community College (NCC) was established on the Navajo Reservation in Arizona. It was the first college on any reservation to be founded and run by Indians, and other tribes soon followed suit. In October 1972, six tribal community colleges formed the American Indian Higher Education Consortium (AIHEC), which today has 30 members in the US and Canada. The AIHEC has proved an effective tool for Indian economic development and the continuance of cultural tradition. Located on or near reservations, the tribal colleges serve more than 20,000 Indian students at any one time in programmes ranging from vocational and technical subjects to post-graduate degrees. Above all, Native colleges place great emphasis on Indian culture. For example, Sinte Gleska College on the Rosebud Sioux Reservation in South Dakota now offers a degree in "Cultural Resources Management", which trains tribal members to collect and manage oral history as well as to locate and protect archaeological and historical sites.

The Navajo Community College (NCC) in Tsaile, Arizona. On the left are a tipi and a traditional Navajo hogan dwelling. The NCC offers a wide range of courses on Navajo culture. For example, students can improve their Navajo language and study traditional curing.

Contemporary curing

European conquest dealt a blow to traditional curing, not least because many Natives fell victim to the new diseases that ravaged their peoples. Traders, missionaries and military doctors first introduced Western-style medical care, and from the early 1800s the US government hired doctors to visit Indian children on reservations and in boarding schools during epidemics. By the 1870s, more than 20 treaties guaranteed some form of medical services to individual tribes. From these arrangements there arose the Indian Health Service (IHS), which today provides primary care on most reservations. Nevertheless, the standard of health care among Indians still lags behind that of the non-Indian population.

However, while many Indians undoubtedly recognize the benefits of Western medicine, its acceptance has varied from nation to nation. Western

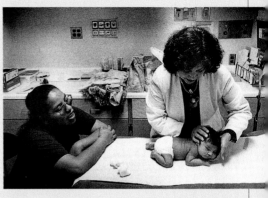

A Choctaw doctor examines a baby at the health centre in Philadelphia, Mississippi, chief town of the Mississippi Choctaw Reservation.

medicine is entirely secular in character, whereas Native curing is associated with holy people (see pp.92–7). For this reason, Western medicine has often been seen as a tool of white oppression, a means of undermining Native culture and spirituality. Over the years, whites have denounced traditional curers as

A Navajo medicine man prepares a sandpainting for a traditional curing ceremony. The patient sits on the painting facing east, which is traditionally the source of blessing. He or she then becomes an actor in the sacred story shown in the sandpainting, which depicts the supernatural beings that have been diagnosed as the source of illness. Taking part in the myth is thought to help to cure the patient by restoring his or her harmonious relationship with the relevant spirits.

witch doctors and ridiculed and condemned their healing methods. As recently as 1976, Christian mission doctors ordered some Navajo families to bring in their medicine bundles to be burned. For many Indians, such attitudes are insulting, patronizing and, above all, sacrilegious. In fact, Native medicine has not been displaced. In most Indian communities, people usually rely on a variety of health care resources, from traditional healers to private non-Indian physicians and government hospitals.

Old Native methods of curing remain important to many people, but the decline in traditional education (see p.146) means that it is more difficult today to train healers (although several Indian educational institutions, such as the Navajo Community College, offer courses). Many communities recognize that they must assume greater responsibility for directing their own health care, and seek an approach that can accommodate traditional methods and values as well as Western medicine.

One way to improve the standards of Indian health care and to decrease the suspicion felt by many toward Western medicine is to increase the number of Native health professionals practising in Indian communities. The IHS funds a programme called Indians into Medicine (InMed), which provides Western medical training for a third of all Indian health care professionals. The IHS is attempting to return control of health care to communities, emphasizing traditional values. For example, Indian holistic healing methods may be the best way to deal with some of the most common maladies that affect Native people, such as diabetes, hypertension and alcoholism. These are considered to be "white man's diseases" that are related more to social factors (that is, lifestyle) than to physiological causes. A return to Native values in treating such problems is the aim of the numerous "Red Road" schemes that have grown up in recent years (see pp.156–7).

HEALING PLANTS

Traditional Indian curers use a wide range of medicinal plants in their healing, and a number of Indian discoveries were adopted by Western medicine. For example, a headache cure made from poplar or willow bark contains the active ingredient salicin, which is used in aspirin. For muscular aches, curers extracted an astringent, later known as witch hazel, from the shrub *Hamamelis*

virginiana. The bark of the shrub *Phamnus purshiana* has been used since 1878 in the most common laxative sold in the US.

Many aromatic plants, such as sage, were used for ritual fumigation. People would "bathe" in the smoke or inhale it for purification. A variety of ailments may be treated with sage infusions.

Salvia columbariae *(left) is a variety of sage used by the Numlaki of California for curing and other purposes.*

Cottage industries to casinos

In the 19th century, the loss of tribal land (see pp.22–5) and the white demand for furs and other goods (see p.40) quickly destroyed traditional Native economies. Dispossessed of land and excluded from the lucrative side of the fur trade, Native people were reduced to working for meagre pay in cottage industries. Skilled woodcarvers made axe-handles, and the weavers of fine baskets made laundry hampers and other domestic containers for whites.

Not every Indian nation saw a decline in its traditional economy. The Northwest Coast peoples still had access to the wealth of the sea, and the Navajo transformed their lands into a rich agricultural area for cattle, sheep and a wide variety of crops. However, many peoples of the forests and Plains, forced to attempt farming on infertile, marginal land in forests and on hot, dry prairies, were left with little prospect but assimilation or starvation.

In 1934, the US government partly awoke to this situation and passed the Indian Reorganization Act (IRA). It allowed Indian nations to conduct their own affairs, enabling them to act as corporations in order to borrow money and operate businesses. Very gradually, and almost always in a hostile climate, Indians began to develop new economic bases that were more in line with the white society that surrounded them.

Today, Native business as a whole is increasing as part of the broader resurgence of Indian self-confidence and pride. Even the arts and crafts industry has spread beyond the tourist stalls, and is now heavily commercialized. However, Native unemployment remains high, approaching 90 percent on some reservations. This situation will radically improve only when there are sufficient numbers of Indian professionals, skilled technicians and entrepreneurs to enable Native people to take complete control of their own economies and compete freely in the marketplace.

NATIVE CASINOS

The most successful Native-owned businesses in the US are casinos. Organized gambling is banned in most states, but Indian reservations are quasi-autonomous and outside state law. Native entrepreneurs have succeeded in creating a highly profitable multi-million-dollar industry. One of the largest and most successful casinos is on the Mashintuquet Pequot Reservation in southeastern Connecticut. In addition to gaming tables, bingo and thousands of slot machines,

A bingo-caller at Grand Casino on the Mille Lacs Ojibway Reservation, Minnesota.

the casino incorporates a 1,500-seat theatre, speciality shops and restaurants. There is even an adjoining hotel.

In accordance with Native North American traditions, the wealth produced by Indian casinos tends to be redistributed among the various Native communities of the reservation. Some tribes prefer to distribute their revenues on a per capita basis. Others have taken a longer-term view and used funds to improve the tribal infrastructure by building schools, roads and museums.

Two Mohawk steelworkers on a building site high above the streets of New York City. The Caughnawage (Kahnawake) Mohawk Reserve in Quebec has profited from the steel industry since 1886. In that year, the Canadian Pacific Railroad recruited Mohawks to work on a bridge across the St Lawrence River, one end of which stood in the reserve. Steel construction was dangerous work – more than 30 Mohawks perished when a half-built bridge near Quebec collapsed in 1907 – but white employers were impressed by the Indians' apparent indifference to heights. Their reputation spread, and many Mohawks and other Iroquois were employed in the construction of most of the steel-framed skyscrapers that dominated the New York skyline after 1900. By the 1960s, a sizeable Mohawk community lived in the city. Mohawk steelmen were also in demand elsewhere in the US: for example, they worked on San Francisco's Golden Gate Bridge.

Tourism

Tourism was an inevitable outgrowth of European expansion westward. For most whites, Indians existed at a distance, always just beyond the frontier settlements. They were regarded as terrifying barbarians who nevertheless possessed a peculiar nobility. It was to satisfy the fascination of a largely urban white public in the eastern US and in Europe that the romanticized "Wild West" was created by 19th-century writers of pulp fiction.

The "Wild West" proved a great tourist attraction. Buffalo hunts, Indian warriors and, of course, heroic white cowboys were all packaged for popular white consumption. Artists such as Karl Bodmer and George Catlin (see p.48) contributed to whites' fascination with their vivid images of Indian life, and photographers such as Edward S. Curtis (see p.105) created set pieces that lent Indian people a haunting beauty that reflected the Victorian preoccupation with the "noble savage". If people could not go to see Indians, the Indians might come to them. William "Buffalo Bill" Cody (1846–1917) hired Native people – including such famous warriors as Sitting Bull (see p.32) – to appear in his immensely popular Wild West Show, which toured America and Europe.

With the advent of "Western" films in the 20th century, the Plains Indian chief, resplendent in eagle-feather warbonnet, was established as the enduring image of the North American Indian. This was what tourists expected to see, and some Native peoples adapted to the popular image in order to make a living. At the turn of the 20th century, tribes across the continent, irrespective of cultural tradition, donned Plains warbonnets to reassure tourists that they and their wares were genuinely Indian. Even today, some Indian men are able to earn a living by

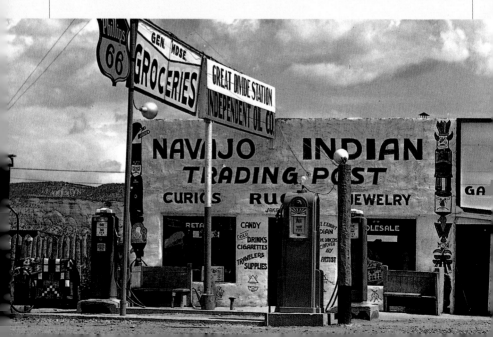

posing for photographs at tourist sites wearing fringed buckskin, beads and feathered headdresses. However, the days are past when entire communities would turn out to stage important tribal dances and ceremonies, such as the Sun Dance, simply as tourist entertainments.

There are positive aspects of tourism. Importantly, Native people are now taking control of the Indian tourist industry. Inuit tour companies offer dog-sledding, nights in an igloo and North Pole expeditions. Visitors to the South Dakota Badlands (see p.79) can stay at a lodge run by the Oglala Sioux and visit a hideaway where Lakota Indians fled from the US Army in 1890.

This store and garage on the Navajo Reservation is adorned with crude images of totem poles, which are a genuine feature only of Northwest Coast cultures. The shop offers "curios", "rugs" and "jewelry" to passing tourists.

TOURIST ART

With the advent of tourism, Native peoples adapted their arts and crafts for a non-Native market. For example, some Southwestern potters switched from making finely finished, elegant pots to crude, primitive designs that looked more "authentic" to visitors. The tourist demand for souvenirs led to the sale of millions of cheap wooden and plastic totem poles, tomahawks and other pseudo-Indian replicas. Most were made in Asian toy factories: Indians have rarely sought to benefit from this lucrative, but low quality, side of the tourist trade. Authentic, handmade arts and crafts are generally more expensive and of higher quality.

However, while tourism has had a negative effect on some Indian arts and crafts traditions, it has ensured that other Native skills and styles have survived into the present. Since the 1960s, Native artists such as Bill Reid (see p.119) and Norval Morrisseau (see p.121), who took the authentic tradition as their starting point, have achieved international fame, and their work commands high prices. Some non-Indians exploited the high-quality Native art market by passing off paintings, sculpture and other popular items as "Indian". In 1990, the US Congress responded with the Indian Arts and Crafts Act, which aimed to prevent non-Indians from marketing imitations of Native work. Controversially, the measure gives Indian tribes control over the definition of a Native artist (see p.11). However, the act should ensure that genuine artistic traditions continue to thrive.

ABOVE *A pincushion (left) and a pouch, made for the white market in the late 19th century by Iroquois artists who employed traditional beading techniques of the Northeast.*

Bear Butte

Rising 4,426 feet (1,350m) above the plains of South Dakota, Bear Butte commands startling views of the Paha Sapa (Black Hills) to the west, while open plains stretch to the eastern horizon. It is revered as a holy place by a number of Plains peoples, including the Lakota Sioux, who call the outcrop Mato Paha ("Bear Hill"), and the Cheyenne, who call it Noavasse ("Medicine Lodge"). Every year, many Lakota and Cheyenne go to the butte for a period of prayer and fasting.

The butte is the focus of conflict with non-Indians who wish to develop the area for tourism and recreation. It forms part of Bear Butte State Park, run by the state of South Dakota. The state closes the summit to visitors during important Indian ceremonies, and prohibits anyone except Indians from using fasting and vision-quest areas and ceremonial trails. However, many Indians maintain that the park authority has desecrated the butte by developing parking lots and campsites on the lower flanks and a tourist climbing trail on the hill itself. Also, despite the safeguards, sacred areas have been violated.

Lakota and Cheyenne spiritual leaders took the state to a federal court under the 1978 American Indian Religious Freedom Act. The court found that Indian interests were outweighed by the state's obligation to improve public access to a geological and historical landmark and to guarantee the safety and welfare of visitors. In 1983, the US Court of Appeals upheld the decision and the Supreme Court refused to hear the case. However, the Cheyenne and Lakota refuse to abandon their fight to secure this and other sacred sites.

BEAR BUTTE •

Pacific
Ocean

North
Atlantic
Ocean

1 *The English name Bear Butte derives from the Lakota, who say that the hill came into existence as the result of a fight between a giant bear and a monster called Unkchegila. The butte marks the spot where the mortally wounded bear lay down and died. The summit of the butte, the highest point for miles around, is a favoured site for* Hanbleceya, *the solitary vision quests (see p.99) of the Lakota. It was here, in 1876, that the famous Lakota chief Crazy Horse is said to have experienced a vision of a bear which gave him supernatural powers. Shortly afterward, Crazy Horse helped to lead the Indian forces that wiped out Custer's troops at the Little Bighorn River (see pp.30–31).*

2
3 *Each of the cloths attached to this pine tree on the summit of the butte represents a prayer to the spirits. Below the tree (3), Indian worshippers also placed tiny pouches of tobacco as sacred offerings. The butte has attracted other worshippers that the Indians find less welcome. In 1994, the Lakota protested against the use of the sacred mountain by "New Agers", who see the butte as a "power point". They conduct summer solstice rituals on the butte that combine Lakota ceremonial with paganism, shamanism and other non-Indian practices that are considered sacrilegious by many Lakota.*

4 *Wesley Whiteman (Black Bear), a Cheyenne holy man, on the summit of Bear Butte in 1977. A bison skull, symbolizing power and strength, is at his feet, and he holds a sack containing a sacred pipe. In Cheyenne tradition, the culture hero Mutsoyef (Sweet Medicine) held a council on the butte that was attended by wise men from all the peoples of the earth. Maiyun, the Great Spirit, gave Mutsoyef four sacred arrows that had great power over buffalo and people.*

The Red Road

In Black Elk's vision (see p.133), a figure called Grandfather speaks of the concept of the "Red Road": "From where the giant lives [north], to where you always face [south], the red road goes, the road of good, and on it your nation shall walk. The red road is a path connecting past and future, a road that is sacred, a road that all people can walk." The Red Road can be understood as the "Indian way". It is an approach to the modern problems of being an Indian that draws upon traditional Native values, such as bravery, spirituality and respect for kin. The Red Road helps to reaffirm Indian identity within the dominant society. Above all, it is a way for Native North Americans to take control of their own destiny.

Many Indian people apply a Red Road approach to modern social problems, such as alcoholism and substance abuse, which affect a large number of families on some reservations. Alcoholism, for example, is a major cause of domestic violence and increased rates of suicide among young Native North Americans. Several Red Road programmes have been developed to tackle these problems. For example, Gene Thin Elk's programme in eastern South Dakota trains counsellors to rehabilitate alcoholics and drug users through retreats and traditional Native teachings and ceremonies. The results have been impressive – Thin Elk's initiative has achieved a greater level of success than Alcoholics Anonymous among communities that have turned to the programme for help.

The Red Road approach has also been applied to the problem of Indian unemployment, which is higher than 85 percent in some communities. The situation remains serious, but local economic development projects guided by traditional Native values of commitment and generosity are proving successful. In the 1980s, the Principal Chief of the Cherokee nation, Wilma P. Mankiller, with her husband, Charlie Soap, set up a system of small business loans and consultancy in order to assist local businesses and co-operatives in

A billboard in Gallup, New Mexico, promotes a brand of wine but bears the warning "Drink Smart or Don't Start". Alcoholism is five times the US average in Gallup, the first big town on the highway out of the Navajo Reservation. Many liquor businesses thrive on trade to Indians. Recently, local Navajos organized a 200-mile (320-km) march from Gallup to Santa Fe, the state capital, to call for more state aid in combating alcoholism and to raise money for Native anti-alcohol programmes.

areas where there was high unemployment and low wages.

Tribal government has also been affected by the revival of Native values. The 1934 Indian Reorganization Act (IRA; see p.150) imposed Euroamerican forms of representative government on tribes, principally in the form of elected tribal councils. Representative democracy often violated traditional forms of consensual government, in which every member of a tribe was directly consulted on important tribal decisions. Today, although all tribes must retain their tribal councils for dealing with the Bureau of Indian Affairs and other federal or state agencies, some Indian nations have sought to return to more traditional forms of tribal government to work alongside the IRA system. For example, the Ihanktonwan (Yankton Sioux) tribe has restored a form of consensual approach, so that all 7,000 enrolled members of the tribe can be directly involved in the drafting of any laws or rules before the tribal council. These range from the allocation of casino revenues and study programmes at the new Ihanktonwan community college, to measures concerned with the preservation of traditional culture.

The often troubled relations between Natives and non-Natives can also benefit from the Red Road. Not all Indians approve the idea of opening sacred traditions and practices to outsiders. But some Natives, such as Lakota holy man Wallace Black Elk (who, while not a blood relative of the earlier Black Elk, considers himself to be a spiritual relative), have worked to foster the Red Road among whites. South Dakota and Minnesota, where relations between Indians and whites have often been tense, have adopted the Red Road as the basis of inter-ethnic reconciliation programmes.

The success of the Red Road initiatives shows that traditional Indian ways remain dynamic and are capable of being applied successfully to the problems of the present day. For many Indians, the Red Road is the key to the survival of Native North American ways of life into the 21st century.

A promotional float for the Native-run alcohol and drug programme on the Cheyenne River Sioux Reservation, South Dakota. The Cheyenne River Sioux have approved a policy aimed at making the reservation completely free of alcohol and narcotics by the end of the 20th century. Elsewhere, alcohol bans have proved highly effective. In the Indian town of Kotzebue, Alaska, a ban on liquor sales led to a 40 percent fall in the number of suicides, murders, assaults and sexual attacks.

Native media

Native North Americans are bombarded daily with stereotyped and frequently negative images of themselves created by non-Indians. The effect of such images is to increase the pressure to assimilate. Therefore, unless the negative imaging can be countered, Native peoples face cultural extinction. As an Indian might put it, the circle – the continuity of Native spirituality and values – will be broken.

Indian people are now trying to halt this trend by developing radio, television, newspapers and other Native media, and by writing their own versions of Native history. At the same time, many Indians are seeking to improve communications among Indian peoples across the North American continent on issues such as Native legal rights and the preservation of cultural heritage. The result, many people

Denise Becenti, a Navajo reporter, conducts an interview for a local television channel serving the Navajo Reservation. Many Indian nations are now served by one or more Native-run television and radio stations. The Native American Journalists Association (NAJA) recently expanded its membership terms to include Native North Americans working in radio and television.

hope, will be an increased understanding of the positive qualities of "Indianness", as defined by Indians and not outsiders.

Priority is given today to the development of Native-run print and electronic media. Ever since the establishment in 1828 of *The Cherokee Phoenix*, North America's first Native newspaper (see pp.45 and 165), there have been continuous efforts by Indians to address the need of their communities for reliable and balanced sources of news and information. In 1984, a group of Native American journalists met to assess the state of the Native media and to discuss ways of developing Native communications. The conference agreed that a national organization was needed to reinvigorate the Indian media, and in particular to address the widespread barriers and challenges that faced Native journalists. They set three goals: an increase in the number of Native journalists; the establishment of training programmes and of support services for Indians already in the field; and an improvement in the general media coverage of Native American issues.

One consequence of the 1984 conference was the establishment of the Native American Journalists Association (NAJA), originally for Native print journalists working in the US. The association launched Project Phoenix, a summer journalism programme for Indian high school pupils, and introduced a national writing competition for high schools. The NAJA recently established a journal, *The Native Voice*. Membership is now open to those in the electronic media and to Native journalists in Canada.

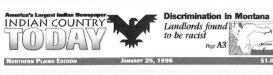

Native publications include intertribal newspapers such as Indian Country Today, *which has the highest circulation of any Native paper, and* The Native Voice, *founded in 1995 at the 11th annual convention of the NAJA in Bismarck, North Dakota. At tribal level, there are newsletters such as the* Cherokee Messenger, *published by the Cherokee Cultural Society of Houston, Texas, and* Akwesasne Notes, *the quarterly magazine of the Kahniakehaka (Mohawk) nation of New York State, Ontario and Quebec.*

INTERNET INDIANS

Artefacts many thousands of years old are mute evidence of active communications networks spanning the North American continent: for example, seashells from the Gulf of Mexico have been found in Manitoba. Where the spoken tongue was a barrier, people developed sign language. Travellers left silent messages – pictographic symbols painted or scratched on rocks, or charcoal marks on birch bark. News could spread very rapidly among tribes along the so-called "moccasin telegraph", passed from person to person by word of mouth.

European settlement broke these traditional lines of communication. However, in the last decade, the fragile unity of Native peoples has received a boost from the development of electronic communications in general and of the Internet in particular. The Internet, a worldwide computer network, has become a potent medium through which Native North Americans can speak to each other and to other indigenous peoples around the world.

The most impressive recent development on the Internet is the World Wide Web (WWW), which offers users cheap and easy access to text, sounds, pictures and even short films through such "websites" as NativeWeb (http://ukanaix.cc.ukans.edu/~marc/nativeweb.html). Accessible worldwide to any Internet user, the WWW provides a steadily growing body of information on Native art, literature, languages, journals, videos, organizations, museums and government resources. Indians and Inuit are using the WWW to tell their own stories and to correct misconceptions about Native cultures. Most importantly, perhaps, the WWW is helping to accelerate the development of pan-Indian – and pan-aboriginal – approaches to common problems that face many First Nations in the modern world.

Documentary Reference

Current land issues

Between 1784 and 1871, Native North Americans ceded nearly two billion acres (810 million ha) to whites in 370 treaties that were often signed under duress or as a result of deliberate trickery. The 1887 Dawes General Allotment Act (see p.25), and amendments to it into the early 1900s, further reduced Indian lands in the US from 139 million acres (56 million ha) to only 34 million acres (14 million ha) by 1934. Nearly half of this area was subject to federal supervision.

Indians went to the courts to seek justice, and their cases clogged the judicial system. The US Congress established the Indian Claims Commission (ICC) in 1946 to hear the claims brought by Native Americans. None of the claims that it investigated were for the return of land, but for financial compensation for lands taken. The ICC sat until 1978, when it was wound up leaving 68 cases unresolved.

Among the most enduring land claims is that of the Western Shoshoni, whose ancestors signed the Treaty of Ruby Valley in 1863. The ancestral land that they are claiming includes a third of the state of Nevada, home to many sensitive government installations. The Shoshoni claim that the Treaty of Ruby Valley did not give their land away, but simply allowed whites to use it. The case was examined by the ICC, which found that the treaty had indeed resulted in the illegal appropriation of 24 million acres (10 million ha) of Shoshoni lands. The ICC offered the people a settlement of about $1.05 per acre (42¢ per ha), the 1863 price. However, the Western Shoshoni have accepted no money for the land because many believe that Mother Earth should not be bought and sold. The Shoshoni are currently seeking a resolution of their territorial claims through an act of Congress.

Similar problems exist in Canada. Among the most tragic, difficult and protracted cases in Canadian legal history is that of the James Bay Cree. They are embroiled in a struggle to protect their lands against the energy company Hydro-Québec, which wants to construct the largest single hydro-electric project in North America. Hydro-Québec has

OPPOSITE *A view of Valley of Fire State Park, part of traditional Indian territory in Nevada. Indian land claims amount to approximately two thirds of the area of the state. The Northern Paiute and Southern Paiute (in whose lands the Valley of Fire stands) claim about a third between them, but the biggest single claim is that of the Western Shoshoni. The 1863 Treaty of Ruby Valley did not dispute Shoshoni rights to the land, but allowed whites to establish a number of ranches, railways and mines there in return for annual payments of $5,000 to the tribe. However, the whites soon abandoned any pretence of abiding by the treaty and simply took over the territory, confining the Western Shoshoni to a number of small reservations.*

already put about 4,400 square miles (11,400km²) of land under water and has allegedly had an ecological impact on another 6,800 square miles (17,600km²). It is said that mercury contamination from decomposing trees and plants affects the fish that are caught and eaten by the Cree, and some elders have been found to have more than 20 times the acceptable level of mercury in their bodies. The government's response has been to advise the Cree to stop eating fish. In 1984, a sudden release of water from the Caniapiscau Reservoir during the migration of the George's River caribou herd drowned more than 10,000 animals. The continuing environmental problems have strengthened Cree opposition to further development and reinforced their demands for more intensive environmental reviews before any new dams are built. The Cree and other Native Canadian groups have persistently called for government intervention, but they remain sceptical and frustrated at the official response.

Some land issues involve disputes between Indian nations, and are rooted in cultural differences, the reservation system and the problems of population growth. The disputes are often complicated by the involvement of government and of energy companies anxious to determine whom they should negotiate with on disputed land. One major argument involves the Hopi and Navajo (Dineh) of the Southwest. The Hopi of Arizona have a traditional land base that overlaps

A dam on Grande-Rivière, Quebec, nears completion. This and other hydro-electric projects pose a great threat to the traditional fishing grounds of the Cree communities of the James Bay area.

that of the Navajo. The Hopi Reservation is completely surrounded by the Navajo Reservation. Each group claimed to
have its origins in the land and viewed it as sacred, and the
treaty of 1882 that created the Hopi Reservation also
promised "protection" for other Indians who lived there. In
1882, there were around 1,800 Hopi and 400 Navajo on the
shared reservation. After 1900, the Navajo population as a
whole grew more sharply than that of the Hopi (in 1900, the
Hopi numbered about 2,000 and the total Navajo population
about 7,500; today, there are 10,000 Hopi and nearly 275,000
Navajo). In 1950, the Navajo on the Hopi Reservation outnumbered the Hopi, and by 1968, tribal tensions between the
traditional enemies were beginning to boil over. In 1974,
Congress intervened to split the peoples by formally parti-
tioning the Hopi Reservation. The Navajo received more
than 900,000 acres (364,000ha) of Hopi land and 400,000
acres (162,000ha) elsewhere to compensate for the land lost
by 5,000 Navajos who were obliged to relocate from the new,
smaller Hopi Reservation. The Hopi lost half their reservation, but only 100 Hopi were obliged to relocate from the
lands given to the Navajo. However, years of legal wrangling,
resistance to relocation by Big Mountain Navajo and constant media attention mean that the controversy is far from
over. The issue has set a precedent for tribes to receive land
instead of money as compensation for lost territory. But
many problems are unresolved, the most important being the
fact that the Hopi have received neither land nor money for
the loss of their lands. The social cost has also been high, in
terms of the upheaval caused especially to relocated Navajo.

   The resolution of one Canadian case stands out as a positive, innovative development in the recognition of Native
land rights. In June 1993, Canada's parliament approved the
Nunavut Land Claim Agreement, which had been ratified by
the Inuit in 1992. A new self-governing territory, Nunavut,
("Our Land" in the Inuit language, Inuktitut), will come into
being early in the 21st century (see map on pp.170–71).
Nunavut is the ancestral home of the Inuit, who have lived in
the eastern and central Arctic for thousands of years. Under
the agreement, they receive title to 136,000 square miles
(350,000km²). The deal gives them more than C$1 billion of
federal funding over 14 years, the right to harvest wildlife
and equal representation on new bodies to manage wildlife,
resources and the environment. They will share federal government royalties from gas, oil and mineral exploration on
Crown lands. The Inuit will control mineral rights on about
ten percent of the land and the right to negotiate with industry on Inuit lands. Three national parks will be created.

Languages

The study of Native languages, most of which were unwritten until very recently, has depended heavily on the often highly unsystematic records of anthropologists, linguists, missionaries and others who came into contact with Indian peoples. As disease and other depredations decimated entire nations, several languages and dialects became extinct. The pressure to assimilate also caused many people to stop speaking their mother tongues. In boarding schools run by churches and government agencies (see p.25), Indian children were often punished for using their first language. However, a considerable number of languages are still spoken by many people – for example, Navajo, which has around 100,000 speakers. In other cases, languages may be spoken by a handful of elders, as in the case of Osage, now the first language of only about half a dozen people.

For such a relatively small Indian population (upward of 1.5 million), there is considerable linguistic diversity. It has been estimated that there may be as many as 300 distinct Indian languages, which may be subdivided further into perhaps 2,000 dialects. The languages can be grouped into at least 57 families, such as Athapaskan, Iroquoian, Muskogean, Salishan and Siouan. California alone is home to 20 language families and is therefore more linguistically diverse than the whole of Europe. A further 17 language families occur west of the Rocky Mountains, with the remaining 20 covering the rest of the North American continent. It is widely accepted by scholars that the 57 families can be grouped into six macro-families, or *phyla*: Eskimo-Aleut, Na-Dene, Macro-Algonquian, Macro-Siouan, Aztec-Tanoan and Hokan. A few scholars go even further and posit a single macro-phylum, "Amerindian", the ancestor of all Native languages. They have sought to relate Amerindian to Asian languages, but most scholars regard Amerindian as too hypothetical for this exercise to be truly fruitful.

This enormous range of languages arose in part from the geographical isolation of many peoples, which led to sharp divergences in related dialects, as among the Tsimshian, whose various dialects are mutually unintelligible. The possibility of several migrations from Asia at different times may also be a factor (see pp.15–16). However, the biggest single reason was the movement of peoples within the continent. Relationships can be detected between the languages of peoples who have ended up as far apart as the Dogrib of the Northwest Territories and the Navajo and Apache of the southwestern US, all of whom speak Athapaskan tongues.

There was much cross-fertilization of languages. Tribes borrowed words from each other and from whites. Some

CHEROKEE PHŒNIX.

GWY · **JᏖ·ᎠᏫᎣ·Ꭺ·**

VOL. I.   NEW ECHOTA, THURSDAY FEBRUARY 21, 1828.   NO. 1.

EDITED BY ELIAS BOUDINOTT.
PRINTED WEEKLY BY
ISAAC H. HARRIS,
FOR THE CHEROKEE NATION.

CONSTITUTION OF THE CHE-
ROKEE NATION,

Formed by a Convention of Delegates from the several Districts, at New Echota, July 1827.

WE, THE REPRESENTATIVES of the people of the CHEROKEE NATION in Convention assembled, in order to establish justice, ensure tranquility, promote our common welfare, and secure to ourselves and our posterity the blessings of liberty; acknowledging with humility and gratitude the goodness of the sovereign Ruler of the Universe, in offering us an opportunity so favorable to the design, and imploring his aid and direction in its accomplishment, do ordain and establish this Constitution for the Government of the Cherokee Nation.

ARTICLE I.

Sec. 1. THE BOUNDARIES of this nation, embracing the lands solemnly guarantied and reserved forever to the Cherokee Nation by the Treaties concluded with the United States, are as follows; and shall forever hereafter remain unalterably the same—to wit:—Beginning on the North Bank of Tennessee River at the upper part of the Chickasaw old fields; thence along the main channel of said river, including all the islands therein, to the mouth of the Hiwassee river, thence up the main channel of said river, including; the islands, to the first hill which closes in on said river, about two miles above Hiwassee old Town; thence along the ridge which divides the wa-

A GOOD CONSCIENCE.

WHAT is there, in all the pomp of

ARTICLE II.

Sec. 1. THE POWER of this Government shall be divided into three distinct departments,—the Legislative, the Executive, and the Judicial.

ARTICLE III.

Sec. 1. THE LEGISLATIVE POWER shall be vested in two distinct branches; a Committee, and a Council; each to have a negative on the other, and both to be styled, the General Council of the Cherokee Nation and the style of their acts and laws shall be,

"RESOLVED by the Committee and Council in General Council convened."

Sec. 2. The Cherokee Nation, as laid off into eight Districts, shall so remain.

Sec. 3. The Committee shall consist of two members from each Dis-trict, and the Council shall consist of three members from each District, to be chosen by the qualified electors of their respective Districts for two years; and the elections to

---

words, such as the Siouan *tipi*, entered the vocabulary of Indians and whites alike. Other Indian words became part of North American English – for example, "powwow" and "caucus". US and Canadian place-names are often of Indian origin, such as Connecticut ("Long River"), Ontario ("Sparkling Water"), Chicago ("Place of Onions") and many other names of provinces, states, towns and physical features. Linguistic borrowing led to the development of lingua francas and hybrids for trade and other purposes. The most famous lingua franca was the Plains Indian sign language. In the Northwest Coast, European words combined with Chinook to form "Chinook Jargon", widely used in trade.

Today, English is the most widespread lingua franca, and indeed has displaced several Native tongues altogether. But many languages are undergoing a revival, including some that were thought to be extinct. For example, Gros Ventre had ceased to be spoken before old recordings of it were found in a museum. Gros Ventre young people are now learning the language. Many Indian schools teach their language as a standard subject, and universities have incorporated Native languages into their curricula. For example, the University of Oklahoma teaches five Indian languages.

The front page of the first issue of The Cherokee Phoenix, *founded in 1828 by Sequoyah, who devised the syllabic Cherokee alphabet (see p.45). The Phoenix, which contained articles in both Cherokee and English, was the first newspaper to appear in a Native North American language. Among those who endeavoured to write down Native tongues were white churchmen who were anxious to propagate the Scriptures. The first Bible produced in any aboriginal language of the Americas was completed in 1663 by John Eliot, an English Protestant minister, in the now extinct Massachuset language of New England.*

Social organization

The stereotypical portrayal of North American Indians includes Eurocentric ideas of the family and of group organization. In fact, such ideas were often imposed on Indian people by missionaries and government officials. In the cinema, Indian families are portrayed as male-centred and nuclear: husbands head the family, couples are monogamous and live with their children within a single dwelling. Tribal organizations are seen as essentially democratic, but headed by a chief who oversees internal affairs and acts as the liaison between the tribe and outsiders.

However, this type of social organization was far from typical. Families were usually not nuclear, but extended, that is, with several generations living in the same household. Nor were marriages usually monogamous: in most Indian groups, a person could have several spouses as long as they could be supported economically. Clan relationships were as important as the individual family and often formed the basis for political structures. Groups were governed in a great variety of ways, ranging from a consensual approach to the "dictatorship" of an all-powerful chief or king, such as the hereditary "Sun Kings" of the Natchez in the Southeast.

Hunting and gathering groups tended to be patriarchal and patrilineal in structure, which meant that males controlled most of the wealth and decision-making, and inheri-

The Algonquian Indian village of Pomeiock on Pamlico Sound in present-day North Carolina, depicted in 1585 by John White. It shows the longhouses that were typical of the eastern woodlands. A longhouse was home to one extended family unit, and a single dwelling might house 30 or more people. White was commissioned to keep a pictorial record of anything "strange to us in England" during the first English expedition to Roanoake Island off the Virginia coast. The result was a collection of vivid, detailed watercolours portraying Native American societies before they were radically changed through contact with the newcomers.

tance was traced through the male line. Many groups of the Plains, Arctic, Subarctic, Plateau and California practised variations on this general pattern. The family unit was typically a patrilineal band of around 15 to 25 people, usually consisting of a man, his wives and their children. The group might also include the man's sons and their families: the extent of the family unit depended largely on what the land could support. Female children married out of the group. Because groups were small, they would band together to form larger units during seasons of abundance in order to carry out rituals, exchange marriage partners and coordinate hunting, warfare, raiding, territorial disputes and other issues. Leadership was usually based on achievement, such as prowess in hunting or warfare. Any status that a leader possessed was accorded only during the time that a group needed his expertise and experience.

Groups that depended on agriculture tended to be matriarchal and matrilineal, with female lines controlling land use and wealth. Some of the farming groups of the Plains, such as the Mandan, and many of the nations of the eastern woodlands fit this general pattern. Family units were large and extended, usually consisting of a woman, her husband or husbands, their daughters and the daughters' families, all living in one residence such as an earthlodge or longhouse. The inheritance of horticultural land, political power and some sacred activities might be traced through female lines. Clans (groups of related families) were sometimes subdivided into halves, or "moieties", which were led by males who traced their ancestry through particular women. Moieties might control sacred bundles (see p.84) and be responsible for organizing warfare or peacetime projects for the whole group. Achievement was valued in a leader, but leadership was based more on ascribed or inherited status. Consensus was a governing principle for group action, but leaders had substantial power to make decisions for the whole group. For certain ritual or secular activities, complex kinship structures frequently worked in tandem with societies that cut across family ties.

An emphasis on social status or even a form of social class structure characterized several groups. For some, status might be based on wealth, but others laid less stress on material possessions. In such cases, status might be related to personal qualities, such as generosity, which most people prized because of its benefits for group survival. Through exchanges and giveaway ceremonies such as the potlatch (see p.62), clans and social groups served as mutual aid societies, ensuring that no one would go without the essentials for survival.

Population 1

Scholars have debated what the aboriginal population of North America might have been before the coming of Europeans. There is, of course, no real way of knowing, but some have tried to calculate numbers using a variety of factors. In the early 1900s, James Mooney of the Smithsonian Institution estimated the pre-contact population of each tribe and came to an overall total of slightly more than a million, a figure that is certainly too low. In the late 1960s, Henry Dobyns used depopulation rates to arrive at a figure of between 9.8 and 12.2 million. In 1983, he recalculated this figure, taking into account the sustaining capacity of the environment, and produced a total of 18 million inhabitants. Douglas Ubelaker and Russell Thornton, among others, have also used depopulation rates, but both have arrived at about 1.8 million people. Thornton now suggests a figure closer to seven million. Future research may bring about a consensus regarding the figure, but meanwhile most experts now accept that the Native North American population on the eve of the arrival of Europeans stood at less than ten million.

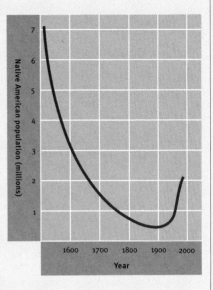

This graph illustrates the steep decline in the Native North American population in the centuries following the first contact with whites, and its subsequent recovery in the 20th century. For the purposes of the graph, the Indian population c.1500 is put at something over seven million.

One fact that most scholars agree upon is the dramatic decline in the Native population due to diseases brought to America by the first Europeans and Africans. Epidemics hit the Indians hard because they had had no prior contact with the illnesses and therefore no bodily immunities against them. Diseases such as smallpox, influenza and measles had the worst effect, often wiping out entire villages. For example, four outbreaks of smallpox and whooping cough between 1781 and 1856 reduced the population of the Arikara, Mandan and Hidatsa, farming villagers living along the Missouri River in the Dakotas, from more than 35,000 to fewer than 2,000. Other diseases, such as typhoid, scarlet fever, diphtheria, mumps and cholera, also claimed many Indian victims.

Disease was the most significant factor in the decline of the Indian population, but warfare and attempted genocide, including forced removals (see pp.22–3), relocation and starvation, also played their part. Not all disease was introduced by accident. For example, in 1763, the British military commander in Pennsylvania deliberately arranged for smallpox-infested blankets to be sent to Indians. Even in the late 20th century, Indian Health Service doctors are said to have performed involuntary sterilization on Indian women. In addition, the general destruction of traditional ways has reduced the effectiveness of traditional curing.

By 1900, the Indian population had fallen to well below one million. Considering the immensity of this decline, Native populations have made a remarkable recovery during the 20th century. In part, this results from better health care. Intermarriage with non-Indians and increased fertility have also led to a higher birthrate for Indians than for the general population. According to the 1990 US census, the population of Indians, Eskimos (this term, rather than Inuit, is still used for census purposes) and Aleuts is close to two million. Taking into account about 740,000 Native Canadians (Indians, Inuit and Métis), the total population of Native North Americans will be approaching three million by the year 2000.

However, present-day figures are difficult to ascertain because of problems associated with identifying who is or is not Indian. The number of people now calling themselves Natives has increased dramatically. According to one estimate, nearly seven million Americans have Indian blood, and the recent popularity of Native North American culture has made more people willing to declare their ancestry. The federal Bureau of Indian Affairs operates a "blood quantum" system whereby a person is usually required to possess at least one Indian grandparent in order to qualify as "Indian" under its rules. But tribes have their own criteria. Some require members to be at least half-Indian by blood, but other tribes will insist only on one Indian great-great grandparent. A few require only documentation of Indian heritage.

In Canada, Indians have to be registered in order to enjoy the recognition accorded under the Indian Act of Canada. A registered Native person is known as a Status Indian. Non-Status Indians are unregistered, either because they have never registered or because they have given up registered status in order to become enfranchised (that is, to possess the same rights as any non-Indian Canadian). The Métis, a group of mixed French-Indian ancestry, are culturally distinct but not yet legally recognized. The US government recognizes more than 300 tribes receiving services from the Bureau of Indian Affairs. About 125 groups are currently seeking recognition, and more will probably do so in the future. In Canada, there are 596 recognized Indian bands.

Indian populations are starting to reflect the trends of the dominant society, although the birthrate still remains slightly higher among Indian people. The most important trend is that of Native people leaving reservations and reserves in order to find work in the cities.

Population 2: Map

This map shows the main areas of Native population in present-day North America. The largest concentrations of Indian peoples in the US are in Oklahoma (the former Indian Territory, to which many tribes were removed; see pp.22–3), California, New Mexico and Arizona. About a quarter of all Indians live on 278 federal and state reservations, in pueblos and rancherias, or on tribal trust lands. The Navajo Reservation has the largest population, with 145,000 Indian residents. About 64,000 (60 percent) of Alaska's Native peoples live in Alaska Native Villages. In Canada, the largest concentrations of registered Indians are in Manitoba, Saskatchewan, British Columbia and Ontario, with about 70 percent living on the 2,272 Canadian government reserves. An increasing number of Indians have moved to urban areas in recent years, mainly to enhance job prospects. In the US, many have been encouraged by government financial incentives to leave the reservations and find employment in the cities.

NEWFOUNDLAND

QUEBEC

PRINCE EDWARD ISLAND

Montreal
VERMONT
MAINE
NOVA SCOTIA

NEW BRUNSWICK

NEW YORK
NEW HAMPSHIRE
MASSACHUSETTS
RHODE ISLAND
CONNECTICUT

Toronto

Buffalo
New York

IGAN

Detroit
PENNSYLVANIA
NEW JERSEY

OHIO
DELAWARE
MARYLAND

WEST VIRGINIA

NTUCKY
VIRGINIA
NORTH CAROLINA

ESSEE

SOUTH CAROLINA

ALABAMA
GEORGIA

FLORIDA
Miami

- Federal reservations (US)
▲ State reservations (US)
∴ Federal reserves (Canada: density of dots indicates density of reserves)
● Major urban Indian populations
□ Province of Nunavut

Glossary

adobe Building material made of earth mixed with straw and baked in the sun; constructed of adobe.

Algonquian A family of languages spoken principally in the Northeast (q.v.) and on the Plains (q.v.); also used to refer to any people speaking an Algonquian language, such as the Algonkin (a people of the Great Lakes region), the Micmac and the Cheyenne. Also spelled Algonkian.

Anasazi An ancient culture of the Southwest (q.v.) that flourished *c*.AD700–1300; of or pertaining to this culture (see p.53).

Arctic The culture area stretching from the eastern tip of Siberia along the northern coastal regions of Alaska and Canada to Greenland. It is the homeland of the Aleut and Inuit peoples (see pp.66–9).

Athapaskan A family of languages spoken principally in the Subarctic (q.v.) and the Southwest (q.v.); also used of any people speaking an Athapaskan language, such as the Beaver and the Navajo. Also spelled Athapascan and Athabascan.

buffalo In this book, "buffalo" always refers to the North American buffalo, or bison.

butte A flat-topped hill, geologically similar to a mesa (q.v.) but covering a smaller area.

California The culture area incorporating most of the present-day state of California in the US and the Baja (Lower) California peninsula in Mexico. It is the homeland of the Hupa, Chumash, Luiseño and other peoples (see pp.58–9).

caribou A large species of deer inhabiting the northern tundra. Also known as reindeer.

corn In this book, "corn" always refers to maize, one of the most widely-grown crops of North America, also known as Indian corn.

culture hero A being which assists humans in their primeval struggles – for example, by bringing them fire and daylight and by killing monsters (see pp.120–23).

earthdiver A being which, in one common type of Native creation myth, dives to the bottom of the primeval waters to retrieve soil, from which the first dry land is then formed (see pp.116–18).

Euroamerican An American of European descent; of or pertaining to European American culture.

Eurocentric Showing a tendency to judge the world in terms of Western (that is, European) values and experiences.

Great Basin The culture area covering a vast desert basin of the western US, bounded on all sides except the southwest by the Rocky Mountains, the Sierra Nevada and other ranges. It is the traditional homeland of the Ute, Paiute, Shoshoni and other peoples (see pp.50–51).

Great Lakes Lakes Erie, Huron, Michigan, Ontario and Superior and the adjacent regions.

hogan A traditional Navajo dwelling, usually constructed of logs and earth or adobe (q.v.).

Iroquoian A family of languages spoken principally in the Northeast (q.v.); also used to refer to any people speaking an Iroquoian language, such as the Iroquois (q.v.) and the Huron.

Iroquois The collective name given to several Iroquoian-speaking peoples of the northeastern US and southeastern Canada. Specifically, it refers to six Iroquois peoples who formed an alliance known as the Iroquois League or the Six Nations (the Cayuga, Mohawk, Oneida, Onondaga, Seneca and Tuscarora; see p.41).

kachina Among the Hopi and other Pueblo (q.v.) peoples, a kachina is a benevolent ancestral spirit or deity. Kachinas participate in important festivals in the form of masked impersonators.

kiva A partly subterranean chamber used for important rituals and ceremonies by the Hopi and other Pueblo (q.v.) peoples. The term is also used for similar structures characteristic of the ancient cultures of the region, such as the Anasazi (q.v.).

longhouse A type of rectangular dwelling that is home to several families. Longhouses were formerly characteristic of the Iroquois and other peoples of the Northeast (q.v.) (see p.166).

medicine bundle A bundle of holy objects that are believed to possess special significance or to be a source of "medicine" (spirit power) for an individual. It is similar to a sacred bundle (q.v.).

mesa A flat-topped elevated region, similar to a plateau but covering a smaller area.

Northeast The culture area encompassing the temperate woodland regions of what are now the northeastern US and southeastern Canada. It is the homeland of most Algonquian and Iroquoian peoples (see pp.38–41).

Northwest Coast The culture area covering a narrow coastal belt extending from northern Alaska down to northern California. It is the homeland of the Tlingit, Haida, Kwakiutl, Tsimshian and other peoples (see pp.60–63).

pan-Indian Of, pertaining to or involving all Indian peoples in general, as in "pan-Indian movement".

Plains or **Great Plains** The culture area covering the great expanse of plains and prairies that form the heartland of the North American continent, stretching from central Canada to Texas and from the Rocky Mountains to the Mississippi River. It is the homeland of many peoples, including the Blackfoot, Mandan and Sioux in the north, the Cheyenne and Pawnee in the centre and the Kiowa and Comanche in the south (see pp.46–9).

pre-contact Of or pertaining to the period before the first contact between Europeans and Native people.

prehistoric Of or pertaining to the time before written historical records, in other words, any period for which our knowledge is based primarily on archaeology. In Native North American terms, this may refer to any time before the arrival of whites.

pueblo (Spanish: "village") 1. A traditional town or village of the Southwest (q.v.) constructed of adobe (q.v.) or stone. 2. (With capital) A people of whom such settlements are characteristic, such as the Hopi and the Taos (see p.53).

sacred bundle A bundle of holy objects that are believed to possess special significance or to be a source of great spirit power for a tribe or group. It is similar to a medicine bundle (q.v.).

Siouan A family of languages spoken principally on the northern Plains (q.v.); also used to refer to any people speaking a Siouan language, such as the Sioux and the Winnebago.

Southeast The culture area covering the southeast of the North American continent, from present-day eastern Texas to Virginia. Like the adjacent Northeast region (q.v.) it is largely forest, but the climate is warmer, wetter and in parts subtropical. It is the traditional homeland of the Cherokee, Creek, Seminole and other peoples (see pp.44–5).

Southwest The culture area that covers the arid lands south of the Great Basin (q.v.) and west of the Plains (q.v.) and extends into northern Mexico. It is the homeland of the Navajo, the Apache and the agrarian Pueblo peoples (q.v.) (see pp.52–5).

Subarctic The culture area stretching the width of northern North America south of the Arctic (q.v.) and east of the Northwest Coast (q.v.). Characterized by lakes, rivers and hardy coniferous forest, it is the homeland of the Kutchin (Gwich'in), Beaver, Cree and other peoples (see pp.64–5).

tipi A conical tent of buffalo hide. It is of Plains (q.v.) origin but was adopted by some other tribes owing to the ease with which it can be dismantled and transported by horse. Also spelled teepee.

wigwam A domed tent of bark or matting, formerly the characteristic dwelling of many Algonquian (q.v.) peoples.

Bibliography

Bierhorst, J. *The Mythology of North America*, William Morrow, New York, 1985

Billard, J.B. *The World of the American Indian*, National Geographic Society, Washington, D.C., 1974

Brody, H. *Maps and Dreams*, Pantheon Books, New York, 1981

Chamberlain, V.D. *When Stars Came Down to Earth, Cosmology of the Skidi Pawnee Indians of North America*, Ballena Press, Los Altos, California, 1982

Champagne, D. (ed.) *Native America: Portrait of the Peoples*, Visible Ink Press, Detroit, Michigan, 1994

Cornell, S. *The Return of the Native, American Indian Political Resurgence*, Oxford University Press, Oxford and New York, 1988

Cove, J.J., and G.F McDonald (eds) *Tsimshian Narratives I: Tricksters, Shamans and Heroes*, Canadian Museum of Civilization, Mercury Series, Ottawa, 1987

Davis, M.B. (ed.) *Native America in the Twentieth Century, an Encyclopedia*, Garland Publishing, Inc., New York and London, England, 1994

Deloria, V. *God is Red, a Native View of Religion*, North American Press, Golden, Connecticut, 1992

DeMallie, R. (ed.) *The Sixth Grandfather, Black Elk's Teachings Given to John G. Neihardt*, University of Nebraska Press, Lincoln, Nebraska, and London, England, 1984

Driver, H.E. *Indians of North America*, University of Chicago Press, Chicago, 1961

Dyck, N., and J. Waldram *Anthropology, Public Policy and Native Peoples in Canada*, McGill-Queen's University Press, Montreal, 1993

Ewers, J.C. *Plains Indian Sculpture*, Smithsonian Books, Washington, D.C., 1986

Fagan, B. *Ancient North America*, Thames and Hudson, London and New York, 1995

Gatuso, John (ed.) *Insight Guide: Native America*, APA Publications, Hong Kong, 1992

Gill, S.D. *Beyond the Primitive, the Religions of Nonliterate Peoples*, Prentice Hall, Englewood Cliffs, New Jersey, 1982

Hardin, T. (ed.) *Legends and Lore of the American Indians*, Barnes and Noble Inc., New York, 1993

Jonaitis, A. *From the Land of the Totem Poles*, American Museum of Natural History, New York, 1988

Josephy, A.M. (ed.) *America in 1492*, Vintage Books, New York, 1993

Kehoe, A.B. *The Ghost Dance, Ethnohistory and Revitalization*, Holt, Rinehart, and Winston, Ft. Worth, Texas, 1989

Kehoe, A.B. *North American Indians, a Comprehensive Account*, Prentice Hall, Englewood Cliffs, New Jersey, 1992

Kopper, P. *The Smithsonian Book of North American Indians Before the Coming of the Europeans*, Smithsonian Books, Washington, D.C., 1986

Krupat, A. *For Those Who Come After, a Study of Native American Autobiography*, University of California Press, Berkeley, California, 1985

Kupferer, H.J. *Ancient Drums, Other Moccasins, Native North American Cultural Adaptation*, Prentice Hall, Englewood Cliffs, New Jersey, 1988

Martin, C. (ed.) *The American Indian and the Problem of History*, Oxford University Press, Oxford, England, and New York, 1987

Maxwell, J.A. (ed.) *America's Fascinating Indian Heritage*, Readers Digest, Pleasantville, New York, 1978

Maurer, E.M. (ed.) *Visions of the People, a Pictorial History*, The Minneapolis Institute of Arts, Minneapolis, 1992

McLuhan, T.C. (ed.) *Touch the Earth: a Self-Portrait of Indian Existence*, Promontory Press, New York, 1971

Murie, James, and D. Parks (eds) "Ceremonies of the Pawnee" (parts 1 & 2), in *Smithsonian Contributions to Anthropology*, Washington, D.C., 1981, vol. 27

Powers, W.K. *Oglala Religion*, University of Nebraska Press, Lincoln, Nebraska, and London, England, 1975

Price, J. *Indians of Canada, Cultural Dynamics*, Sheffield Publishing Company, Salem, Wisconsin, 1988

Ridington, R. *Trail to Heaven, Knowledge and Narrative in a Northern Native Community*, University of Iowa Press, Iowa City, Iowa, 1988

Schlesier, K.H. *Plains Indians, AD500–1500, the Archaeological Past of Historic Groups*, University of Oklahoma Press, Norman, Oklahoma, and London, England, 1994.

Sturtevant, W.C. (gen. ed.) *Handbook of North American Indians*, Smithsonian Institution Press, Washington, D.C., 1981

Trimble, S. *The People, Indians of the American Southwest*, School for American Research Press, Santa Fe, New Mexico, 1993

Vastokas, J.M., and R.K. Vastokas *Sacred Art of the Algonkians*, Mansard Press, Peterborough, Ontario, 1973

Waldman, Carl *Atlas of the North American Indian*, Facts on File, New York, 1984

Wallace, A.F.C. *The Death and Rebirth of the Seneca*, Vintage, New York, 1972

Weatherford, J. *Indian Givers. How the Indians of the Americas Transformed the World*, Fawcett Columbine, New York, 1988

Weatherford, J. *Native Roots, How the Indians Enriched America*, Fawcett Columbine, New York, 1991

Will, G.F., and G.E. Hyde *Corn Among the Indians of the Upper Missouri*, University of Nebraska Press, Lincoln, Nebraska, and London, England, 1917

Woodhead, H. (series ed.) *The American Indians*, Time-Life Books, Richmond, Virginia, 1994

Index

Picture credits

The publisher thanks the photographers and organizations for their kind permission to reproduce the following photographs in this book:

Abbreviations
T top; C centre; B bottom; L left; R right

1 Werner Forman Archive; **2** National Anthropological Archives, Smithsonian Institution; **6–7** Darwin Wiggett/First Light

The First American Peoples
8–9 Jack Parsons; **10** Werner Forman Archive/Portland Art Museum; **11L** US Army Military History Institute; **11R** US Army Military History Institute; **13T** Sheldon Preston; **13B** Peter Furst; **15** Denver Museum of Natural History; **16** e.t.archive; **18–19** (1) Cahokia Mounds Historic Site; (3) Paul Devereux; (4) Cahokia Mounds Historic Site; (5) Cahokia Mounds Historic Site/photo by Pete Bostrom

Dispossession
20–21 Huntington Library, California; **24** Nebraska State Historical Society/John Anderson Collection; **25** Private Collection; **26** Stephen Trimble; **27** Idaho State Historical Society; **28** Frank Spooner Pictures/Gerard Kosicki; **29T** Mary Evans Picture Library; **29B** Rochester Museum & Science Center; **30** Courtesy of the Southwest Museum, Los Angeles/Photo #CT.1; **31** Peter Newark's Western Americana; **32** Library of Congress; **33** Corbis/Bettman; **34** National Anthropological Archives, Smithsonian Institution; **35** Wide World/Associated Press

Lands and Peoples
36–7 *Alone with the Past* by Roland Reed/Kramer Gallery, Minneapolis; **39** Library of Congress; **41T** School of American Research/photo Rod Hook; **42–3** (1) J.A. Kraulis/Masterfile; (2) Bill Brooks/Masterfile; (3) Bill Brooks/Masterfile; (4) Alan Marsh/First Light; **45T** Library of Congress; **45B** from *The Indian Tribes of North America* by Thomas McKenney and James Hall, 1860; **47** Sumner W. Matteson/Milwaukee Public Museum; **48** Bridgeman Art Library; **49** America Hurrah, NYC; **51** The Burns Archive; **53** Stephen Trimble; **54** Rex Features; **55** Stephen Trimble; **56–7** (1) Jack Parsons; (3) Thomas Maxwell; (4) Paul Devereux; **59T** *Captain John*, The Brooklyn

Museum Archives, Culin Archival Collection, Expedition Reports, 1905, Augustus W. Erickson; **59B** America Hurrah, NYC; **61** Neg. No. 42298 (Photo by Edward Dossetter) courtesy of the Department of Library Services/American Museum of Natural History; **62** National Museum of the American Indian, Smithsonian Institution/photo David Heald; **63L** American Museum of Natural History, Smithsonian Institution/Stephen Meyers; **63R** American Museum of Natural History, Smithsonian Institution/Department of Library Services; **65** Sherman Hines/Masterfile; **66** Bryan & Cherry Alexander; **69** Bryan & Cherry Alexander; **70L** America Hurrah, NYC; **70R** Stephen Trimble; **71C** British Museum/Museum of Mankind; **72L** America Hurrah, NYC; **72BR** America Hurrah, NYC; **73L** America Hurrah, NYC

The Life of the Spirit
74–5 Lois Ellen Frank/First Light; **76** Thomas Maxwell; **77B** Photograph by Richard Collier, Wyoming Dept of Commerce; **78** Peter Furst; **79T** Peter Furst; **79B** Michael Crummett; **80** e.t.archive; **81** Thomas Maxwell; **82–3** (1) Royal Anthropological Institute, London; (2) James McGuire/Ursus Photography; (3) James McGuire/Ursus Photography; (4) John K.B. Ford/Ursus Photography; **84** Neg. No. 3847 (Photo by Stephen S. Myers) courtesy Department Library Services/American Museum of Natural History; **85** Peter Furst; **86–7** H.F. Robinson, courtesy Museum of New Mexico/ Neg. No. 21603; **88B** Amerind Foundation, Dragoon, AZ; **89** Owen Seumptewa, Native Shadows, 1994; **90** Michael Melford; **92** Werner Forman Archive/Museum of the American Indian, Heye Foundation; **93** Library of Congress; **95** American Museum of Natural History; **97** Susanne Page; **98** Richard Erdoes; **99** Michael Crummett; **100** Werner Forman Archive; **101** Wheelwright Museum of American Art/Herb Lotz; **102** Milwaukee Public Museum; **103** Peabody Museum/Harvard University; **104** Paul Stafford/Minnesota Office of Tourism; **105** Smithsonian Institution; **106–7** (1) Ohio Historical Society; (3) C.C. Lockwood/Animals Animals; (4) Ohio Historical Society; **108** Stephen Trimble; **109** Ashmolean Museum, Oxford; **110** Murv Jacob; **112** Rex Features; **113** *Cheyenne Sundance* by Dick West/Philbrook Museum of Art, Tulsa

Sacred History
115 Nebraska State Historical Society/John
Anderson Collection; 117T Rochester Museum &
Science Center, Rochester, New York; 117B Peter
Furst; 118 Wheelwright Museum of the American
Indian; 119T Thomas Maxwell; 119B University
of British Columbia Museum of Anthropology/
carving by Bill Reid; 121 *Windigo* by Norval
Morrisseau/Glenbow Museum, Calgary; 122
Courtesy of The Burke Memorial Washington
State Museum/Cat. No.117a; 123B John Bigelow
Taylor, NYC/New York State Historical
Association @ Clare and Eugene Thaw
Collection; 124 Robert Harding Picture Library;
125 Musée de l'Homme, Paris/collection M.
Delaplanche

The Survival of the Sacred
126–7 Monty Roessel; 128–9 Stephen Trimble;
130 Rochester Museum & Science Center,
Rochester, New York; 132 Private Collection;
133T Peter Furst; 133B National Anthropological
Archives, Smithsonian Institution; 134 from *The
Indian Tribes of North America* by Thomas
McKenney and James Hall, 1860; 135 C. Hart
Merriam/Phoebe Hearst Museum of
Anthropology; 136–7 National Anthropological
Archives, Smithsonian Institution/Bureau of
American Ethnology Collection; 137T Thaw
Collection, Fenimore House Museum,
Cooperstown, New York/photo John Bigelow
Taylor

To the Seventh Generation
138–9 John Running; 140–41 Michal Heron;
142–3 Frank Spooner Picture Library/
Westernberger Liaison; 144 AP/Wide World; 145L
US Army Corps of Engineers, Omaha District;
145R State Archaeological Research Center/South
Dakota State Historical Society; 146–7 Monty
Roessel; 148T Ed Kashi; 148B Michal Heron; 149
Courtesy of the Hunt Institute for Botanical
Documentation, Carnegie Mellon University,
Pittsburgh, PA; 150 Courtesy of Grand Casino,
Mille Lacs; 151 David Grant Noble; 152–3 Ferenz
Fedor/Courtesy of the Museum of New Mexico/
Neg. No.102015 History; 153T & B Patterson
Graphics, Inc./Dayton Museum of Natural
History; 154–5 (1) South Dakota Tourism; (2)
Michael Crummett (3) Michael Crummett; (4)
Warren Schwartz/Courtesy of the Center for
Western Studies, Augustana College, Sioux Falls,

South Dakota; 156 Elaine Querry; 159 Courtesy
of *Indian Country Today*, *The Native Voice*,
Cherokee Messenger and Audie Griffin, designer,
The Cherokee Cultural Society of Houston,
Akwesasne Notes

Documentary Reference
160 Bill Brooks/Masterfile; 162 Peter
Christopher/Masterfile; 165 Courtesy of the
American Antiquarian Society; 166 e.t. archive

Commissioned artwork:
12 Hugh Dixon; 14, 18 (2), 22–3, 38, 43, 44, 46,
50, 52, 56–7 (2), 58, 60, 64, 68, 83, 107 (2), 155
Line + Line; 16–17, 41, 67, 77, 88, 95, 96, 101,
109, 120, 122–3, 131 Gillie Newman